STOCKTON

Renewed, Revitalized, Redefined

Stockton Arena

STOCKTON

Renewed, Revitalized, Redefined

ANNE GONZALES

This book was produced in cooperation with the Greater Stockton Chamber of Commerce. Cherbo Publishing Group gratefully acknowledges this important contribution to *Stockton: Renewed, Revitalized, Redefined.*

cherbo publishing group, inc.

president	JACK C. CHERBO
chief operating officer	ELAINE HOFFMAN
editorial director	CHRISTINA M. BEAUSANG
managing feature editor	MARGARET L. MARTIN
feature editor	JO ELLEN KRUMM
senior profiles editor	J. KELLEY YOUNGER
profiles editors	NEVAIR KABAKIAN
	LIZA YETENEKIAN SMITH
associate editors	SYLVIA EMRICH-TOMA
	JENNY KORNFELD
editorial assistant/proofreader	MARK K. NISHIMURA
profiles writers	B. D. CAMPBELL
	SYLVIA EMRICH-TOMA
	NEVAIR KABAKIAN
	JENNY KORNFELD
	JO ELLEN KRUMM
	TERRAN LAMP
creative director	PERI A. HOLGUIN
senior designer	THEODORE E. YEAGER
designer	NELSON CAMPOS
senior photo editor	WALTER MLADINA
photo editor	KAREN MAZE
digital color specialist	ART VASQUEZ
sales administrator	JOAN K. BAKER
client services supervisor	PATRICIA DE LEONARD
senior client services coordinator	LESLIE E. SHAW
client services coordinator	KENYA HICKS
executive assistant	JUDY ROBITSCHEK
administrative assistant	BILL WAY
western regional manager	BART B. BARICA

Cherbo Publishing Group, Inc.
Encino, California 91316
© 2008 by Cherbo Publishing Group, Inc.
All rights reserved. Published 2008.

Printed in Canada
By Friesens

Subsidiary Production Office
Santa Rosa, CA, USA
888.340.6049

Library of Congress Cataloging-in-Publication data
Gonzales, Anne
A pictorial guide highlighting Stockton's
economic and social advantages.

Library of Congress Control Number 2008938143
ISBN 978-1-882933-09-9
Visit the CPG Web site at www.cherbopub.com.

To purchase additional copies of this book, contact Joan Baker at Cherbo Publishing Group: jbaker@cherbopub.com or phone 818.783.0040 ext. 27.

Dedication

This book is for Stockton's residents, past and present, who believe in their city. Through their vision, pioneer spirit, creativity, and hard work, they made Stockton a place where dreams can come true, a place to work, relax, reinvent, and build a life, a place to call home.

Acknowledgments

I want to thank the Greater Stockton Chamber of Commerce and its Conference and Visitors Bureau, the City of Stockton Office of Economic Development, the San Joaquin Partnership, and the Downtown Stockton Alliance, along with Stockton's business, arts and entertainment, education, and professional communities, all of which contributed to this project. Every day, these gracious people invest themselves into making Stockton a city with promise for the future. I am also grateful to my family and friends for encouraging me to write, and to all my English teachers and professors throughout the years, who consistently urge generations of writers to find their voices and use them.

— Anne Gonzales

The landmark historic Klamath Ferry, home to Duraflame

The Stockton leg of the 2007 Amgen Tour of California

TABLE OF CONTENTS

On the building: STOCKTON MEMORIAL CIVIC AUDITORIUM

TOMORROW AND FOREVER, THE PEOPLE OF STOCKTON WILL HOLD IN MEMORY THE VALOR OF
WHO ON LAND AND SEA, AT HOME AND ABROAD, SERVED THEIR COUNTRY IN DEFENSE O

From left to right: The restored Bob Hope Theatre; the historic 1916 Belding Building downtown; the Stockton Memorial Civic Auditorium.

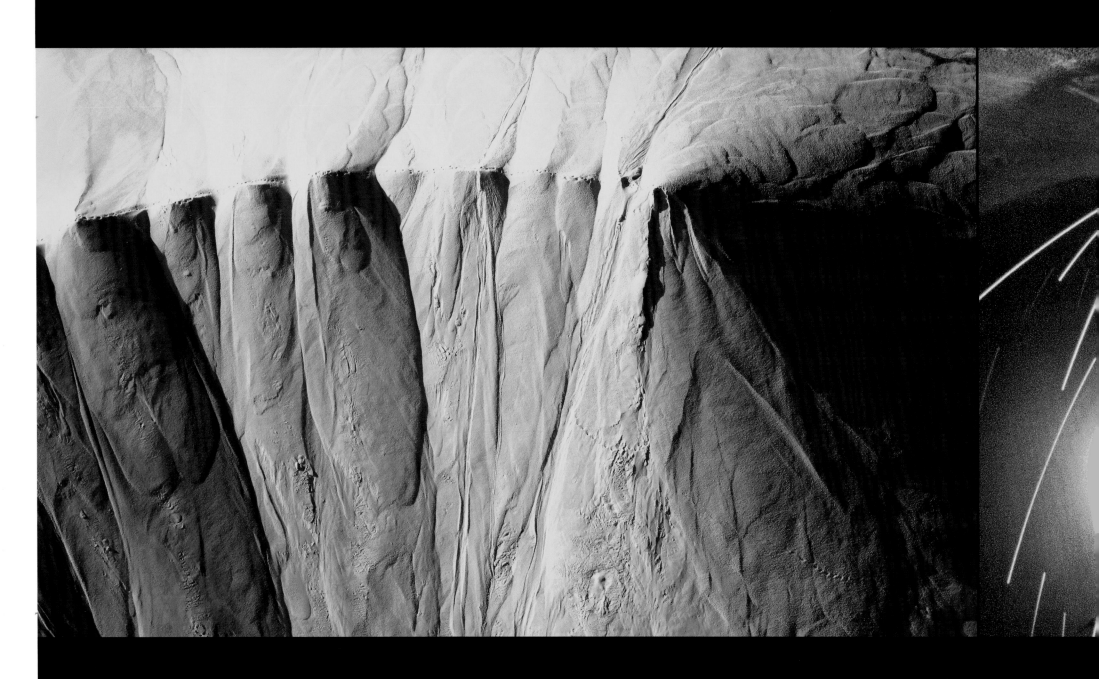

From left to right: Sulfur, the top outbound commodity of the Port of Stockton in 2007; a welder at work in a Stockton aqueduct; a bulk hauler near Stockton.

From left to right: The Empire Theatre on Stockton's Miracle Mile; the Downtown Art Walk; the Brubeck Institute Jazz Quintet at the University of the Pacific.

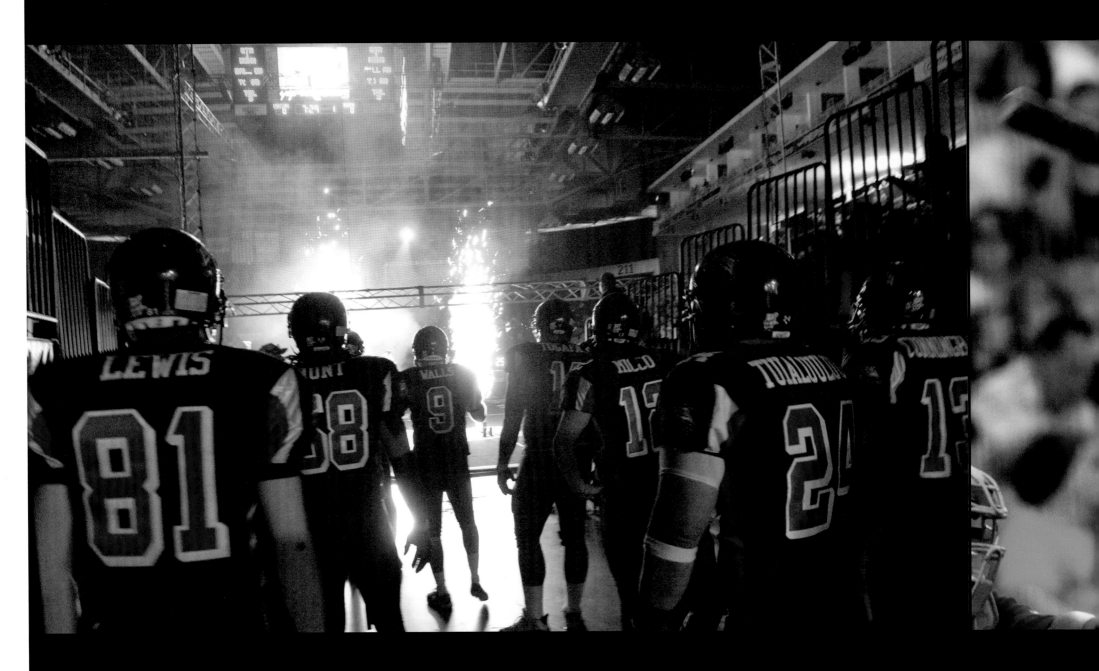

From left to right: The Stockton Lightning arena football team; the Stockton Ports baseball team; the Stockton Thunder ice hockey team.

From left to right: The Children's Museum of Stockton; the Haggin Museum; python and guests at the zoo in Micke Grove Park.

CORPORATIONS & ORGANIZATIONS PROFILED

The following organizations have made a valuable commitment to the quality of this publication.

Port of Stockton

BUSINESS VISIONARIES

The following companies and organizations are recognized as innovators in their fields and have played a prominent role in this publication, as they have in the region.

Ace Tomato Co., Inc.
2771 East French Camp Road, Manteca, CA 95336
Phone: 209-982-5691 / Fax: 209-982-0235
Web site: www.lagorio.com
"Pride in every phase of our operation"

Neumiller & Beardslee, A Professional Corporation
509 West Weber Avenue, Fifth Floor, Stockton, CA 95203
Clifford W. Stevens, President
Phone: 209-948-8200 / Fax: 209-948-4910
E-mail: cstevens@neumiller.com
Web site: www.neumiller.com
"Lawyers Who Find Solutions"

Bank of Stockton
Business Address: 301 East Miner Avenue, Stockton, CA 95202
Mailing Address: P.O. Box 1110, Stockton, CA 95201
Contact: Angela Brusa, Vice President and Director of Marketing
Phone: 209-929-1445 / Fax: 209-929-1434
E-mail: angelabrusa@bankofstockton.com
Web site: www.bankofstockton.com
"A History Apart from the Rest"

Port of Stockton
2201 West Washington Street, Stockton, CA 95203
Contact: Richard Aschieris, Port Director
Phone: 209-946-0246 or 800-344-3213 / Fax: 209-465-7244
E-mail: portmail@stocktonport.com
Web site: www.portofstockton.com
"Stockton and the Central Valley Gateway to the World"

Iacopi, Lenz & Company, Accountancy Corporation
3031 West March Lane, Suite 300 East, Stockton, CA 95219
John T. Iacopi, CPA; Susan H. Lenz, CPA
Phone: 209-957-3691 / Fax: 209-957-0841
Web site: www.iacopi.com

San Joaquin Delta College
5151 Pacific Avenue, Stockton, CA 95207
Contact: Greg Greenwood, Director of
Public Information and Marketing
Phone: 209-954-5051 / Fax: 209-954-5860
E-mail: greggreenwood@deltacollege.edu
Web site: www.deltacollege.edu
"Your Future Begins at San Joaquin Delta College."

J. R. Simplot Company
999 Main Street, Boise, ID 83702
P.O. Box 27, Boise, ID 83707
Phone: 208-336-2110
E-mail: jrs_info@simplot.com
Web site: www.simplot.com

San Joaquin County Employment & Economic Development Department
San Joaquin County WorkNet
56 South Lincoln Street, Stockton, CA 95203
Contact: John Solis, Executive Director
Phone: 888-512-WORK (888-512-9675) within California; or
209-468-3500 outside California / Fax: 209-462-9063
E-mail: info@sjcworknet.org
Web site: www.sjcworknet.org
"A Foundation for Success"

San Joaquin Partnership, Inc.
2800 West March Lane, Suite 470, Stockton, CA 95219
Michael E. Locke, President and CEO
Phone: 209-956-3380 / Fax: 209-956-1520
E-mail: mlocke@sjpnet.org
Web site: www.sjpnet.org
"A Single Source for All Your Location Needs"

St. Joseph's Medical Center
A member of CHW

St. Joseph's Medical Center
1800 North California Street, Stockton, CA 95204
Phone: 209-943-2000
Web site: www.StJosephsCares.org

University of the Pacific
3601 Pacific Avenue, Stockton, CA 95211
Phone: 209-946-2011
Web site: www.pacific.edu
"The West's Most Distinctive, Student-centered National University"

From left to right: Janet Leigh Plaza at night; a beauty boutique on the Miracle Mile; downtown Stockton nightlife.

From left to right: A signpost on the Lodi Wine Trail; wine grapes ready for harvest; entertainment at the Vino Piazza in Lockeford.

From left to right: Victory Park; flying over the San Joaquin Delta at sunrise; playing in the fountain at Micke Grove Park near Lodi.

From left to right: Stockton's annual Fourth of July celebration at Weber Point; a mariachi band at a Cinco de Mayo event; Gordon Medlin, cofounder of Stockton's long-running Asparagus Festival.

From left to right: Agriculture, a major enterprise on the Delta; Stockton's popular downtown farmers' market; almonds, one of the region's biggest crops.

Aerial view of Weber Point during Stockton's annual Asparagus Festival

FOREWORD

As a fifth-generation Stocktonian and CEO of the 107-year-old Greater Stockton Chamber of Commerce, it gives me great pleasure to welcome residents and visitors alike to the pages of *Stockton: Renewed, Revitalized, Redefined*.

Stockton has a proud history beginning prior to the Great Gold Rush, an exciting present, and a very bright future due to the fact that throughout the years the people of Stockton believe what is here cannot be duplicated anyplace else. It is this uniqueness that sets us apart from other communities.

Stockton was founded by Captain Charles M. Weber, and on July 23, 1850, the city was incorporated. Stockton is the county seat of San Joaquin County, one of the original 27 counties established that year in the new state of California. This fertile county has been and continues to be the supplier of abundant agricultural products to California, the nation, and the world.

Stockton currently ranks as California's 13th-largest city in population and the 62nd-largest city in America. Our diverse population represents and showcases people from around the world and is one of the city's strongest attributes. Stockton was named "All-America City" in 1999 and 2004!

Add that to our central location, weather, the Delta that leads to our inland deepwater seaport, our revitalized downtown, and many other wonderful residential and business districts and you have a wonderful place to live and visit. We truly have a city that is on the move and the jewel of the valley that will grow brighter and brighter as the years go on.

Cities around the country certainly face challenges in our ever-changing society, but the people of Stockton have a well-established feeling of COMMUNITY and confidence. They are working together to allow those now here to enjoy the quality of life that all deserve and are preparing for those who will come in the future so they can enjoy the rich history of Stockton and, at the same time, make a lasting and exciting history of their own.

Sit back and enjoy the past, live the now, and dream of the wonderful future Stocktonians have before them!

Doug Wilhoit
Chief Executive Officer

GREATER STOCKTON
CHAMBER OF COMMERCE

STOCKTON TIMELINE

1849   1853   1876   1893

Charles M. Weber, founder of Stockton

1849
German immigrant Charles Weber names his fledgling town, established on part of a Mexican land grant, after Commodore Robert Stockton, a hero of the recent Mexican-American War.

1849
During the California Gold Rush, thousands arrive in Stockton, a gateway to the goldfields located between the Mokelumne and Merced rivers.

1850
Henry Radcliffe and John White publish the town's first newspaper, the *Stockton Times*.

1850
Stockton is officially incorporated as a city.

1851
Charles Weber donates land for the Temple Israel Cemetery for Stockton's Jewish community. It is the oldest Jewish cemetery in continuous use in California.

1853
The Insane Asylum of California is founded. It is the state's first public hospital to treat mentally ill patients.

1862
Massive floods hit throughout the state. In Stockton, all bridges are destroyed and many streets are under water when levees on the Mormon Slough break.

1867
Stockton Savings and Loan Society, which later will become the Bank of Stockton, is founded.

1869
The first Western Pacific train, carrying visitors from Sacramento, arrives in Stockton.

1870
Ambrose Randall establishes the town's first high school.

1876
St. Agnes Academy, a Catholic girls school run by Dominican Sisters, opens.

1880
Stockton is home to the third-largest Chinese community in California.

1881
City founder Charles Weber dies of pneumonia at the age of 67.

1887
The California Well Company lays natural gas pipelines throughout the city, making Stockton the first California city to be supplied with natural gas.

1888
The *San Francisco Daily Examiner* publishes Ernest Thayer's poem "Casey at the Bat." Many Stocktonians believe their city (nicknamed "Mudville") and baseball team were the inspirations for the poem.

1893
The construction of a new county jail is completed. The jail is nicknamed Cunningham's Castle for its fortress-like design and the town's sheriff, Thomas Cunningham.

1895
The *Stockton Evening Record* newspaper begins publication. The paper later will be known as *The Record*.

1895
On Lock Sam, which would become a popular and long-lived Cantonese restaurant in the city, opens its doors on Washington Street.

1896
John Humphreys assumes academic administration duties at the Stockton Business College, Normal School, and Telegraphic Institute. The college later will be renamed Humphreys College.

1899   1904   1919   1925

1899

St. Joseph's Home and Hospital (now St. Joseph's Medical Center) opens with 25 hospital beds under the supervision of the Dominican Sisters of San Rafael.

1904

Benjamin Holt tests a steam-powered machine that moves on self-laying tracks instead of wheels. He names the crawler tractor the Caterpillar.

1904

Stockton High School is built at the corner of California and Vine streets.

1908

The Stockton Terminal and Eastern Railroad provides rail freight service in the greater Stockton area.

1910

The Hotel Stockton, featuring 252 rooms and 200 private baths, opens.

1919

Roy Allen mixes up a batch of creamy root beer and sells it in Lodi, launching A&W Root Beer.

1920

After reclaiming 29,000 acres of uncultivated land, George Shima controls 80 percent of California's potato market. He is later nicknamed the "Potato King."

1921

KWG Radio begins transmissions.

1923

The College of the Pacific, the state's first chartered institution of higher education, moves from San Jose to Stockton.

1925

The Stockton Memorial Civic Auditorium, dedicated to the Stockton soldiers who died in World War I, is completed.

1925

Charlie Chaplin's film *The Gold Rush*, which features scenes in Stockton, is released. Stockton later will appear in more than 70 films.

Manlio Silva, founder of Stockton Symphony

1926

Violinist and conductor Manlio Silva founds the Stockton Symphony, the third-oldest orchestra in California.

1929

Congress approves federal funding to deepen the San Joaquin River to create the Stockton Deepwater Ship Channel.

Benjamin Holt, left, greeting General Ernest Swinton at the Holt offices, Stockton, 1918

STOCKTON TIMELINE

1930   1940   1945   1957

The Fox California Theatre, 1938

1930

The Fox California Theatre opens in downtown Stockton. Approximately 20,000 people attend the opening celebration, which features the latest "talkie" movies and comedy skits.

1931

The Louis Terah Haggin Memorial Galleries and San Joaquin Pioneer and Historical Museum officially opens. The institution later will be known as the Haggin Museum.

1933

The Port of Stockton, the first inland seaport in California, opens.

1935

Tillie Lewis opens the first Flotill Products cannery, which processes American-grown Italian tomatoes, in Stockton. Lewis is later nicknamed the "Tomato Queen."

1940

Author Maxine Hong Kingston, who will write *The Woman Warrior* and other books, is born in Stockton.

1942

Jazz pianist and composer Dave Brubeck graduates from the College of the Pacific.

Dave Brubeck

1944

The Naval Supply Annex Stockton is built on Rough and Ready Island. The facility is operated as an annex to the Naval Supply Depot in Oakland.

1945

The Stockton Empire Theatre opens on Pacific Avenue's Miracle Mile.

1948

Stockton Junior College moves from the College of the Pacific campus and is renamed Stockton College. It will later become San Joaquin Delta College.

1956

Singer-songwriter Chris Isaak ("Wicked Game") is born in Stockton.

1956

St. Mary's High School moves to its present location, 5648 North El Dorado Street.

1957

Don Bowden runs a mile in three minutes, 58.7 seconds at the Pacific Amateur Athletic Union Meet in Stockton, becoming the first U.S. runner to complete a mile in less than four minutes.

1961

The College of the Pacific changes its name to the University of the Pacific.

1966

The San Joaquin County Historical Museum is established in Micke Grove Regional Park near Lodi.

1967　1993　2001　2008

1967

A fountain is built as the centerpiece for the redesigned Hunter Square.

1974

California State University at Stanislaus opens its Stockton Development Center on the San Joaquin Delta College campus.

1979

Interstate 5 opens from Stockton to Sacramento. The freeway is built to allow traffic to travel from northern to southern California without using Highway 99.

1986

The first Stockton Asparagus Festival, a three-day food and entertainment celebration, is held.

1993

Stockton's Crosstown Freeway, which links California Highway 99 with Interstate 5, is completed.

1998

The Stockton Development Center, renamed California State University, Stanislaus–Stockton Center, moves to Magnolia Avenue.

2000

The University of the Pacific establishes the Brubeck Institute, honoring jazz legend Dave Brubeck and his wife, Iola.

2000

During construction of downtown's City Centre Cinemas, workers uncover relics of a laundry and other artifacts from a Chinese community of the late 1800s.

2001

Passenger service at the Stockton Metropolitan Airport begins.

2002

Sunset magazine names Stockton one of the West's best places to live.

2004

The Fox California is renovated and renamed the Bob Hope Theatre. The theater showcases live performances and movie screenings.

2004

Stockton is designated an All-America City by the National Civic League for the second time.

2005

The Stockton Ballpark and Stockton Arena both open. The ballpark is home to the Stockton Ports baseball team. The arena hosts Stockton Thunder hockey, Stockton Lightning arena football, and California Cougars indoor soccer and is a major entertainment venue.

2008

Stephanie Brown-Trafton of Taft wins a gold medal in the women's discus at the Olympics in Beijing, China. Her throw is 212 feet, five inches.

Stephanie Brown-Trafton, 2008 Olympic gold medalist

PART ONE
LIVING, WORKING, AND ENJOYING THE GOOD LIFE IN STOCKTON

CHAPTER ONE

A GREAT PLACE TO CALL HOME
Stockton Living

For people looking for a place to call home, Stockton is a rare mix of big-city opportunities and a friendly, small-town feel. While its history includes California's Gold Rush, Stockton's greatest treasures today are its easygoing living style, its colorful cultural diversity, the great outdoors, a commitment to the arts, varied sports and entertainment, and a wide array of housing, career, and educational options. Stocktonians know how to get down to business, but they also know how to relax and have a good time.

The Stockton area is a place where people can always find something to do, or get away from it all. It is only a few hours from world-class tourist destinations and business hubs, but without the crowds and traffic congestion of other metropolitan cities. Stockton has plenty to attract businesses, but the quality of life makes people stay. The city has comfortable, affordable living space, respected educational institutions, a bounty of outdoor recreation activities, and a tapestry of cultures. While Stockton's businesses, housing, and education are its lifeblood, the city pulses with a thriving arts community and a vibrant sports and entertainment scene. Residents have many choices for work and play, for growth and learning, and for involvement in the community. Stockton is a city of verdant green parks and open spaces; colorful food, music, and festivals; winding Delta waterways; thrilling sports teams and venues; and abundant community activities.

One of the fastest-growing communities in the state, Stockton is currently California's 13th-largest city, with a population of more than 287,000. Stockton is the seat of San Joaquin County, a bustling area in which nonfarm employment is projected to grow almost 2.3 percent annually through 2014. The county is forecast to expand its government, education and health, retail, manufacturing, wholesale trade, professional and business services, and leisure and hospitality sectors, diversifying and stabilizing its traditional agriculture-based economy.

The city celebrates its diversity. Since its days as a Gold Rush outpost, Stockton has pulsated with many ethnic cultures, including Hispanic, Chinese, Japanese, African-American, Southeast Asian, and Filipino. The community's ethnic diversity is reflected today in the names of its streets, its many festivals, and even its grocery stores. Stockton has many authentic stores and restaurants, which include expansive Hispanic shopping centers, tortilla factories, Asian supermarkets, seafood markets, and produce stores.

Stockton has received accolades for its attributes. With more than 100,000 trees, the city has been recognized by *Sunset* magazine as the "Best Tree City" in the western United States. For its efforts to reinvent itself, the city was named an All-America City by the National Civic League in 1999 and 2004.

Gracious living is the norm, with a housing stock that includes historical neighborhoods and upscale homes along waterways. In general, home prices are about a third the cost of those in the nearby San Francisco Bay area. Typical housing prices in San Joaquin County are among the lowest in the Central Valley region, with the average price about $245,000 in May 2008, compared with a $339,000 median price statewide.

The weather is usually moderate in the Stockton area, with its winters mildly crisp and summers warm and dry. The nearby Sacramento–San Joaquin Delta typically produces cooling breezes, making it attractive for summertime outdoor activities and perfect for growing grapes for the area's thriving wine industry.

A Major Events Center

A truly impressive venue for arts, sports, and community events is the Stockton Events Center, a sweeping glass-and-metal structure hugging the city's downtown waterfront. The complex, which opened in 2005, includes the 10,000-seat Stockton Arena, the Stockton Ballpark at Banner Island, a seven-story parking garage, and the Sheraton Stockton Hotel at Regent Pointe, with 179 guest rooms and suites, conference rooms, and a restaurant.

Several professional sports teams are based in Stockton. The arena is home to the California Cougars soccer team; the Stockton Thunder, an East Coast Hockey League (ECHL) team; and the Stockton Lightning, an Arena2 football team. The Stockton Ports baseball team, a minor-league affiliate of the Oakland Athletics, plays at the gleaming Stockton Ballpark at Banner Island.

Downtown Renewal

The Stockton Arena—site of concerts, ballets, circuses, and other events—is one anchor of the downtown waterfront redevelopment effort. The other anchor is the historic Hotel Stockton, a 1910 building at the head of the Stockton Channel, renovated into residential units and retail establishments.

The revitalization project also includes the 16-screen City Centre Cinemas, surrounded by retail and restaurants, and the Bob Hope Theatre, opened as the Fox California Theatre in 1930 and remodeled and renamed after one of the country's favorite entertainers. It hosts concerts, comedy, and Broadway musicals.

Taking advantage of population growth and an economic boom in the city, Stockton is actively revitalizing its downtown core while complementing existing development with bold office projects, new homes, and exciting shops, restaurants, and entertainment spaces. The city seeks to create a pedestrian-friendly, 24-hour downtown community for work, entertainment, and living. Downtown has become a thriving entertainment district with a variety of live performances, sports events, dining, shopping, strolling, art galleries, and special events. A measure of the popularity of the district is the more than 4,000 people a week who come to the downtown farmers' market each Friday from May through October to shop for seasonal local produce, nuts, desserts, and ciders, along with crafts.

Stockton is also in the midst of a downtown residential renaissance as the city focuses on reviving charming, historic, tree-lined neighborhoods. The city has strong infill and rehabilitation programs that support building and remodeling in older sections. The city offers incentives for building in the downtown sector, including reduced or eliminated fees and redevelopment grants, while giving help to businesses wanting to improve building facades.

The Downtown Stockton Alliance, an improvement association for the city's central core, works enthusiastically to make downtown a top destination for residents and visitors. It actively recruits new businesses to locate downtown and organizes numerous special events, such as Art Walks, that draw crowds to the center of the city. The alliance's guides provide hospitality and security for the area, and the alliance also provides additional maintenance to keep downtown clean and tidy. The alliance and the city's Office of Economic Development recently launched a downtown Stockton marketing plan to promote Stockton as a world-class city and business and tourism destination.

A City of Parks and Festivals

Outdoor activities await at the city's 63 parks, ranging from small neighborhood sites to a 64-acre community park. The city observes summer with a free concert series in historic Victory Park, and concertgoers are encouraged to bring their picnic baskets, blankets, and lawn chairs to enjoy an evening of live music under majestic oaks. The city is dotted with golf courses, baseball and softball fields, tennis courts, soccer fields, skateboard parks, and public swimming pools. Stockton also boasts an Olympic-size ice rink, Oak Park Ice Arena, for both competitive and leisure ice-skating and hockey.

Stockton is always ready for a fiesta, whether it's the Delta boat parade, the Veterans Day observance, the annual Fourth of July fireworks show, or its many food and craft festivals. The popular Asparagus Festival is the county's largest fund-raiser. More than 110,000 people attended in 2008 to raise $462,000 for more than 100 local charities. Stockton's many ethnic cultures add their own dash to the city's arts and entertainment environment, with such observances as Cinco de Mayo; African-American Juneteenth events; Cambodian, Chinese, and Vietnamese New Year celebrations; the Japanese Obon festival; the Greek Festival; and the Jewish Food Festival. The arts are continually celebrated here, with art in public places and art walks including local art displays, performances, and exhibits at several downtown venues.

Cultural Offerings

The city has a wonderful array of cultural organizations and events. The Stockton Civic Theatre has a jam-packed schedule of live plays and musicals. The Stockton Symphony, founded in 1926, is the third-oldest orchestra in California, and performs everything from the classics to jazz. The Stockton Opera, in its 39th season, performs at a concert hall at the University of the Pacific in Stockton.

The International San Joaquin Film Festival debuted in 2008 with more than 44 films from 14 countries, with screenings and galas held at several venues, including the Bob Hope Theatre, the Empire Theatre, and the University of the Pacific.

Set in Stockton's Victory Park, the Haggin Museum has both fine art and history collections, including exhibits from Stockton history as well as an Egyptian mummy. One exhibit features artifacts from an 1870s Chinese laundry excavated in downtown Stockton in 2000. The museum, opened in 1931, has grown to 34,000 square feet of exhibit space.

Stockton has two enthralling destinations for children. Pixie Woods in Louis Park is a playland in a fairy-tale setting with a merry-go-round and boat and train rides. It has been a landmark for over 50 years. The Children's Museum of Stockton, on Weber Avenue downtown, combines learning with play in hands-on exhibits inside its tiny town.

For knowledge-seekers of all ages, a central library and its 12 branches in the
area offer access to books, articles, databases, and Web sites. Weekly events
range from puppet shows and small-business seminars to family movies and
children's science programs.

Shopping Destinations

Shoppers in Stockton can choose from a wide range of delightful shopping districts and dynamic malls. For fashion, food, home decorations, accessories, and
gifts, Stockton's retail scene has it all. Two large adjacent malls, Weberstown
and Sherwood, create an exciting destination for shoppers. Weberstown is
anchored by Dillard's, JCPenney, and Sears, while Sherwood features a variety
of department stores, such as Macy's, Gottschalks, and HomeGoods, as well
as pet, electronic, jewelry, and fashion stores.

For a more relaxed atmosphere, shoppers can stroll through Stonecreek Village,
a new open-air collection of upscale shops nestled among stone pathways and
refreshing water fountains. Lincoln Center, a dining and shopping mainstay in
the heart of Stockton since 1951, has 91 shops and 12 restaurants ranging from
casual to gourmet.

Miracle Mile is a historic, pedestrian-friendly collection of specialty shops and restaurants on several blocks in the charming Tuxedo Park area. The object of many years of renovation and economic incentives, Miracle Mile has become a hot spot for retail and service, including longtime businesses and boutiques, a farmers' market, after-hours dining at eateries and coffeehouses, live music, and moviegoing at the 1945-era Empire Theatre.

Delights of the Delta

The Stockton area is bursting with recreational opportunities. The city is perched on the shores of the Sacramento–San Joaquin Delta, a 1,000-mile network of navigable creeks and sloughs. Whether residents and visitors like to boat, fish, water-ski, sail, camp, picnic, bird-watch, or just savor a dish of steaming Delta crawdads at one of the colorful eateries nestled on the banks, the rivers and sloughs are a magnet for outdoor enthusiasts and lazy water watchers alike. The Delta's many marinas offer snug harbors for boats, with some offering riverboat excursion tours, water-sports rentals, and fishing supplies. The Stockton Sailing Club, started in 1933 and based in a secure harbor at the Delta, is a resource for racing, lessons, and get-togethers for sailing enthusiasts.

Annual festivals, wine tastings, and food fairs, including the Taste of the Delta and the Isleton Crawdad Festival, celebrate the natural resources of the waterways. The Ryde Hotel, an opulent establishment built in 1927, and the Grand Island Mansion, a 58-room Italian Renaissance estate dating to 1917, offer dining and lodging in the Delta. Both are reminders of a bygone era when celebrities, such as actor Clark Gable and mystery author Erle Stanley Gardner, stayed there, sometimes arriving by riverboat.

Stockton's location makes it ideal for day trips to some of the most scenic and historic destinations in the world, including San Francisco, Lake Tahoe, Yosemite National Park, and locales on the Pacific Ocean. It is also about 50 miles south of Sacramento, California's capital.

A Business-Friendly Climate
Stockton and the surrounding region provide an environment conducive to business development. San Joaquin County is strategically located with interstates, railways, and Stockton's unique deepwater port. The availability and relatively lower cost of commercial and industrial land make Stockton attractive to manufacturers and as a site for distribution centers.

More important to many businesses, however, is the Stockton area's skilled and semiskilled labor force. Employees are able to work for less than their large-city counterparts because living is more affordable in Stockton. Many who commute to the San Francisco or San Jose areas would prefer to work close to home.

For companies considering moving to or expanding in the Stockton area, government agencies and the business community offer considerable assistance in planning, site research, staffing, and financial aid. Stockton is zoned for success as one of a handful of areas in the state with an enterprise zone, aimed at fostering the start of new businesses and expanding existing ones. Locating in an enterprise zone qualifies a business for significant state tax credits; reduced permit fees; help with development and employee recruitment; utility tax rebates; and local, state, and federal financing packages. The California State Enterprise Zone for San Joaquin County was recently conditionally expanded to cover more than 638 square miles, including a large part of Stockton.

This page: Waterfront homes, one of the area's housing options. Opposite page, left: Corto Olive's modern olive-oil processing plant near Lodi; opposite page, right: Brookside Business Park in northwest Stockton.

The City of Stockton, committed to reducing its carbon footprint, encourages environmentally friendly green industries and green building practices. Businesses looking to relocate or expand can view available commercial and industrial sites through Advantage Stockton, an online geographic information system that includes mapping, aerial views, and photographs. The service is offered by the city's Office of Economic Development, which also advises businesses about the permit process to help new businesses get up and running quickly.

The San Joaquin Partnership, a nonprofit economic development corporation, encourages businesses to locate in the county. Its services include industrial and commercial site selection assistance, analysis of development fees and utility costs, support with hiring, and site tours. Since its founding in 1991, it has aided in the creation of a cumulative total of more than 49,000 new jobs, bringing $2.2 billion in labor income to Stockton area workers. One of the partnership's major accomplishments was the creation of a cluster of 10 automobile parts manufacturers that supply the New United Motor Manufacturing, Inc. (NUMMI) plant in Fremont, California.

The Greater Stockton Chamber of Commerce has many programs to give local businesses a boost in their day-to-day operations and to improve the economic climate in Stockton. The chamber's Government Relations Council monitors state and local politics to protect the long-term health of Stockton's business community, while other chamber groups offer forums for discussing the concerns of certain small businesses and industries.

The San Joaquin County Employment and Economic Development Department (SJC EEDD) offers many services to businesses and workers, including recruitment and job placement through the SJC WorkNet division. The San Joaquin County Economic Development Association works with EEDD, local governments, and chambers of commerce to serve as a one-stop resource for such functions as applying for business loans, hiring employees, and obtaining permits.

Stockton's main energy utility, Pacific Gas and Electric (PG&E), offers business services, rebates, incentives, and energy rate analyses. At the PG&E Energy Training Center in Stockton, businesses, construction professionals, and others can get education and hands-on training in energy efficient technology.

For water availability, the Stockton East Water District (SEWD) supplies water to three local water retailers—the City of Stockton, San Joaquin County, and the California Water Service Company. SEWD plans far ahead to protect and increase the availability of this resource and has partnered with the U.S. Army Corps of Engineers and local water agencies on a plan to replenish groundwater.

Stockton brings together an abundance of economic, cultural, educational, and recreational opportunities. It is a great place to work, to live, and to do business, as it is strategically positioned to take advantage of the economic changes and new efficiencies of the 21st century.

CHAPTER TWO

FROM TRADITIONAL TO HIGH-TECH
Manufacturing

The Stockton area has a diversity of manufacturing, with companies making everything from fireplace logs to spacecraft components. Some manufacturing plants are an outgrowth of longtime businesses and the area's agricultural underpinnings, while others are start-ups and expansions, including high-tech firms. All build on the region's legacy of innovation. More than 23,000 people work in manufacturing in the region, according to the U.S. Bureau of Labor Statistics, and the number is growing.

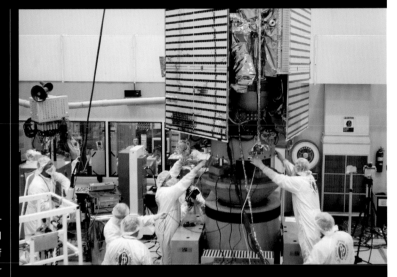

Affordable land, a skilled labor pool, and transportation networks are just a few of the attributes allowing manufacturers to succeed in Stockton. In the past decade, tracts of land have been converted to industrial and warehouse distribution sites, grouped around major freeways, the airport, railroads, and the Port of Stockton, allowing Stockton to balance its farming heritage with job creation and visionary growth. Manufacturers also receive help through local and state economic development and redevelopment money.

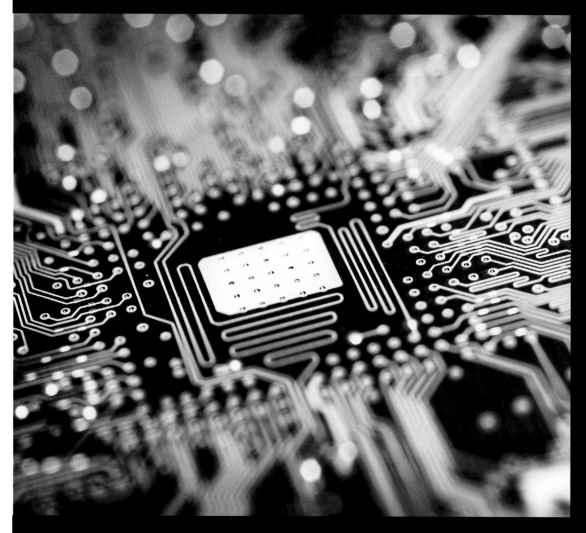

The range of businesses making and selling products is a testament to
Stockton's diversity and sustainability. From automobile parts to cereal, from circuit boards to lumber boards, Stockton area manufacturers make the products
that keep the nation—and many parts of the world—running. Stockton is also
home to manufacturing research laboratories and training centers.

From Sawdust to Success

California Cedar Products is one success story. In 1968, the company was
looking for a way to recycle sawdust from its Stockton pencil-making plant.
Engineers there hit upon mixing the shavings with wax, creating the first
Duraflame log. This convenient and cleaner-burning log revolutionized fireplace use. Today, from its corporate headquarters at the historic Klamath Ferry
in Stockton and three other plants in California, Kentucky, and Ontario,
Canada, Duraflame produces America's leading brand of fire logs, fire starters,
and barbecue products.

Strategic Automobile Parts Location

San Joaquin County is becoming a major supplier of components to the New
United Motor Manufacturing, Inc. (NUMMI) plant in Fremont, California, about
65 miles southwest of Stockton. The Stockton area location allows for a concept called "just in time" manufacturing, in which suppliers produce and ship
just the materials needed for the next day's production.

In 2008, the large Japanese automobile parts manufacturer Aisin Seiki opened its $10 million door-frame production factory in Stockton, employing 60 people. Another Aisin plant, Aisin Electronics, has been in operation in Stockton since 1996, mainly manufacturing sensors for seat positioners, antilock brake systems, and transmissions. Both plants supply NUMMI.

Also in 2008, Kyoho Manufacturing opened its plant on Highway 99 and Farmington Road. Two shifts produce some 11,000 pressed and welded parts each day to go into Toyota Corollas and Pontiac Vibes at the NUMMI plant. The San Joaquin Partnership, an economic development organization involved in bringing the manufacturers to the area, noted that 10 plants in the county, employing more than 2,000 people, supplied components to NUMMI.

Building Better Construction Products

Simpson Strong-Tie, which began making structural connectors in 1956 and now has a full line of products to fortify buildings, has a production plant in Stockton as well as a research facility. The parent company, Simpson Manufacturing, headquartered in Pleasanton, California, is a $500 million business with 2,000 employees and 11 branches in California, Canada, Denmark, the United Kingdom, and France.

To learn how to make buildings even stronger, Simpson Strong-Tie launched its Tyrell Gilb Research Laboratory in Stockton. The laboratory tests structures' ability to withstand earthquakes, high winds, and other natural disasters. Named in memory of an architecture professor who headed the company's research and development efforts for 35 years, the Stockton laboratory has seismic shake tables and rigs to apply pressure to walls. The testing allows the company to craft new structural design technology that will improve building safety and ultimately help save lives.

Stockton is one of 10 North American locations for Custom Building Products, which manufactures tile-setting grout and adhesives, such as epoxies, cement, household and industrial glues, sealants, resins, putties, and latex. Also serving the construction industry is Golden State Lumber, which expanded from the Bay Area into an 80-acre plant in Stockton to serve the building boom of the 1980s. Today, Golden State has a total of five facilities in Northern California.

This page: Rolled steel from Feralloy. Opposite page: Concrete tile shingles made by Eagle Roofing Products.

Feralloy rolled into Stockton with its 150,000-square-foot Western Division hub, serviced by four overhead cranes with a lifting capacity of 30 tons. The company makes rolled and coated steel. Eagle Roofing Products, a division of Burlingame Industries, opened a new plant in Stockton in 2004. The automated, high-speed plant manufactures concrete roof tiles. With a capacity to produce enough tile to cover 60,000 homes a year, the Stockton facility will supply products for Eagle Roofing's new marketing effort into the Pacific Northwest.

Going High-Tech

Stockton is well suited to high-tech and aeronautic companies, many of which came to the Central Valley from the San Francisco Bay area for affordable land and a better quality of life for their workers. One company, Applied Aerospace Structures, selected Stockton because of the city's strategic location between the Bay Area and Sacramento. The company makes lightweight structures for the military and for the commercial aerospace industry, including satellite structures, solar panels for spacecraft, and radar structures for land-based missile guidance systems.

Bay Area Circuits, a 30-year-old business based in Redwood City, has a plant in Stockton for making printed circuit boards.

New Fuels

Community Fuels, a biodiesel production company, leased space for its 40,000-square-foot plant at the Port of Stockton in 2006. Biodiesel is a domestic, renewable fuel for diesel engines derived from natural oils, such as soybeans, and the nation's fastest-growing alternative fuel. The goal of Community Fuels is to build a regional production model for distributing clean, renewable energy.

Food Services and Bottling

With its agricultural base, Stockton is a natural locale for food-related manufacturing plants to thrive. Dopaco, a subsidiary of Cascades, is a global food-service packaging company with a plant in Stockton. It manufactures a variety of paper and plastic foodservice packaging products throughout North America, including folding cartons, beverage cups and lids, carriers, nested cartons, food trays, clamshells, and paper plates. It also serves customers in Asia and Australia through its joint venture, D&D.

This page: Martin-Brower products, keeping McDonald's supplied throughout the region. Opposite page, left: Wheaties, one product from the General Mills plant in Lodi; opposite page, right: Molli Coolz new Stockton plant for making frozen treats.

Martin-Brower, with a plant in Stockton, started providing paper products to the first McDonald's restaurant in 1954. Today it supplies 9,000 McDonald's stores around the globe with everything they need, from beef to fries to operating supplies.

Buhler Sortex in Stockton makes and distributes electronic sensors for food-processing lines, including equipment to sort for color, size, and shape. Another Stockton manufacturer, Vinotheque Wine Cellars, crafts wine refrigeration and storage cabinets.

General Mills, well known for its bakery and other food products, has a plant in nearby Lodi that produces cereal and packaged foods. A major employer in the city, the food company is involved in the community, providing scholarships, sponsoring events, and otherwise aiding local causes.

Stockton became a cooler place when Molli Coolz moved its headquarters from Livermore to a 30,000-square-foot Stockton plant in 2006. The manufacturer uses patented technology to produce beads of cryogenically frozen ice cream and sherbet. The relocation of the company's plant will allow Molli Coolz to boost annual production from two million units to nine million units. The frozen treats are made from cream and natural flavors, and the free-flowing beads are packaged into single-serving cups for retail sales from carts and vending machines and at sports events.

Niagara Bottling, a nationally known water bottler and distributor, built a 162,000-square-foot facility in south Stockton in 2006, with eventual employment expected to be 200.

Whether a plant is making automobile parts, spacecraft components, or frozen treats, Stockton's strategic location, available space, and ready workforce make it a logical choice for modern manufacturing.

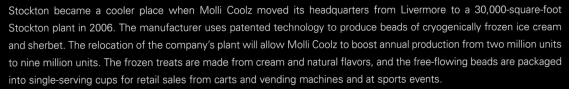

This page: Benefiting from Stockton's many health care options.

Opposite page: A study group at the University of the Pacific.

CHAPTER THREE

NURTURING MINDS AND BODIES
Education and Health Care

For families and individuals in Stockton, the region's dynamic educational programs and quality health care enrich and protect, adding opportunity and vitality for productive, fulfilling lives. Stockton's schools and colleges open doors for students and workers to earn higher degrees, hone their skills, and advance their careers. For elementary and secondary education, the Stockton area has four major school districts—Stockton, Lincoln, Lodi, and Manteca unified school districts—and more than 30 private schools. Several alternative education programs round out the menu of school selections. For higher education and technical training, Stockton has a number of options.

First in the State

One of the best-known universities in the area is Stockton's University of the Pacific. The state's first chartered institution of higher learning, Pacific was founded in 1851 in Santa Clara, moved to San Jose in 1871, and to Stockton in 1923. The private university has more than 6,000 undergraduate and graduate students at its Stockton campus, its McGeorge School of Law in Sacramento, and its Arthur A. Dugoni School of Dentistry in San Francisco.

Its Stockton campus has seven schools, including education, pharmacy and health sciences, business, international studies, engineering, and a conservatory of music. The university offers more than 80 majors and programs. Its accelerated professional degree programs are designed to help dedicated and talented students with high academic ranking and good scores on standardized tests earn a professional degree in a shorter time. The accelerated programs include the health sciences, business, education, and law.

Pacific's Stockton campus is lush with expansive lawns and trees, and the school's chapel is the site of stylish weddings and celebrations. Because of its Ivy League appearance, the campus has been featured in many Hollywood movies, most notably in *Raiders of the Lost Ark*. Accomplished jazz pianist and composer Dave Brubeck is a 1942 graduate of Pacific who eventually became a cultural diplomat for the U.S. government. In 2000, the university founded the Brubeck Institute, which hosts the annual Brubeck Festival.

Many Choices in Higher Education

California State University, Stanislaus (CSU Stanislaus) opened its Stockton center in 1974 and in 1998 moved to the spacious grounds of the former Stockton Developmental Center in the city's central historic district. The CSU Stanislaus–Stockton Center has computer laboratories, a library access center, health services, a fitness center, a student lounge, and landscaped courtyards.

The center offers upper division and graduate courses, including online courses, that lead to bachelor's and master's degrees and one doctorate, as well as to professional credentials. Degree programs include business administration, education, nursing, child development, history, communication studies, and criminal justice. Many students can complete coursework in Stockton without having to transfer to the main campus in Turlock.

The area's largest college in terms of enrollment, San Joaquin Delta College, begun in 1935, offers career and technical training, general education classes, and credits transferable to four-year institutions. Located on 165 acres in Stockton, with courses also offered in outlying communities, the school has over 20,000 students. More than 100 certificate and degree programs, including online courses and degrees, range from accounting to health occupations, and from agriculture to equipment technician. The community college, which has educational partnerships with both Pacific and the California State University system, has an electron microscopy program and houses the George H. Clever Planetarium.

Also located in Stockton is Humphreys College and School of Law. Founded in 1896, the small, private college specializes in business administration, computer science, and law. It offers associate's, bachelor's, and juris doctor degrees.

Exceptional Health Care

Stockton also takes care of its residents through its nurturing network of physicians, medical groups, and hospitals. The area is served by three hospitals and several health-maintenance organizations. Many health clinics offer affordable family medical care, and the county delivers a wide range of services and information on care issues from alcoholism and mental health to public and environmental health.

St. Joseph's Medical Center, the largest regional medical facility in the county, began in 1899 with beds for 25 patients. Today, it has 294 beds, more than 400 physicians, and over 2,400 employees. In addition to its medical, surgical, and diagnostic services, St. Joseph's has a women's and children's center, a regional cancer center, an outpatient surgery facility, and an emergency department. In 2008, its heart center received a HealthGrades excellence award for cardiac surgery.

St. Joseph's is currently building a 152,000-square-foot, four-story patient pavilion, at an estimated cost of $115 million. The construction project includes a new women's and children's center and maternity unit, a neonatal intensive care unit, an adult intensive care unit, 78 new beds, an underground parking garage, and a second-story walking bridge connecting the new building to the existing medical center. Completion is scheduled for spring 2010.

St. Joseph's reaches out to the uninsured and underinsured in many ways. Its CareVan, for example, brings health care, including child immunizations, to different locations in the community. Its Mobile Mammography Unit provides breast-cancer detection in 22 counties of the Central Valley.

Special Deliveries

Stockton's Dameron Hospital, founded as a 20-bed facility by Dr. John Dameron in 1912, is now a 188-bed community hospital. With more than 1,200 employees, the hospital is one of the largest employers in San Joaquin County. It provides acute care, emergency medicine, surgery, cardiology, home health, occupational therapy, and other services. Dameron, which delivers many babies at its Start of Life maternity center, received a HealthGrades Maternity Care Excellence Award for 2007–08.

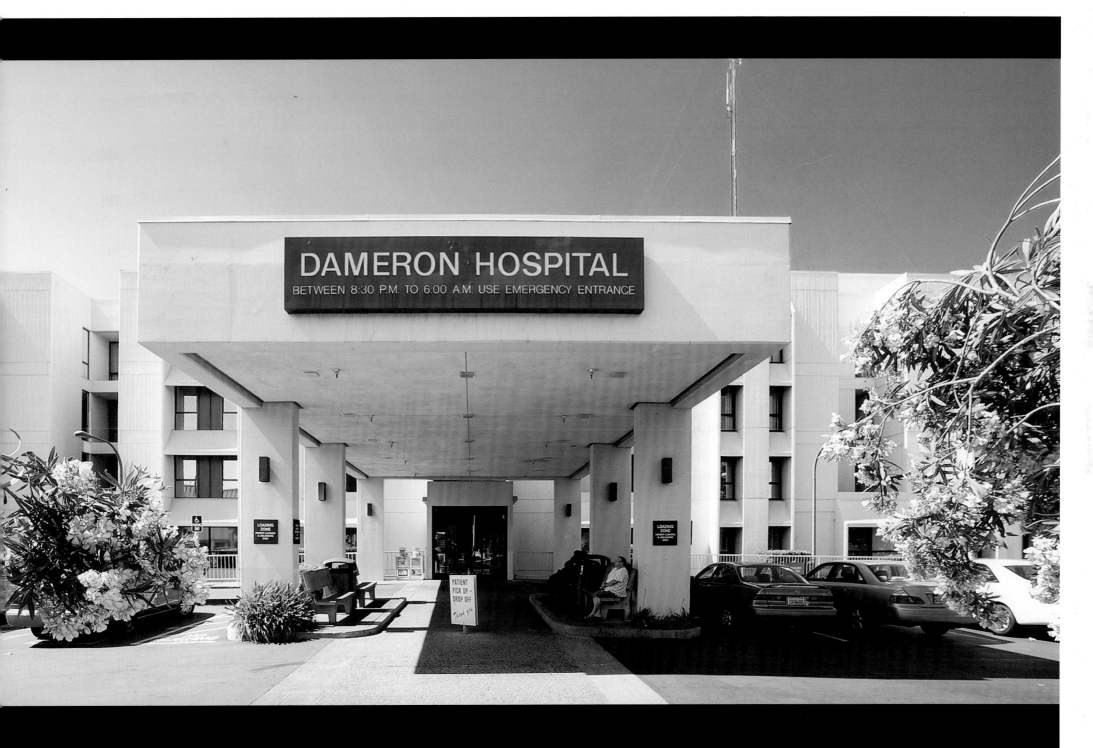

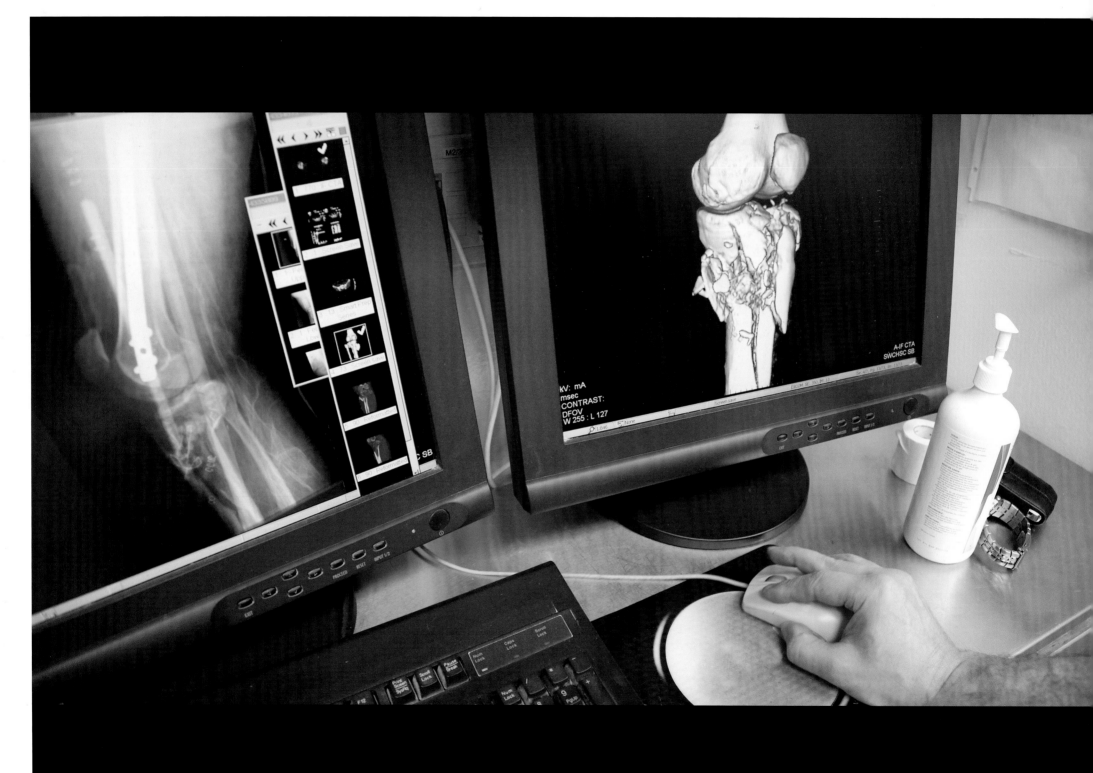

Caring for All

San Joaquin General Hospital in nearby French Camp is a 236-bed facility founded in 1857. The hospital's inpatient care includes general medical and surgical care, high-risk obstetrics, neonatal intensive care, pediatrics, acute physical medicine, and rehabilitation. The hospital has 11 provider sites throughout the county, providing more than 200,000 outpatient clinic visits a year. The county-owned hospital is involved in a number of training programs, including physician residency, registered and licensed vocational nursing, pharmacy, and radiologic technology.

The nation's largest nonprofit health plan, Kaiser Permanente, offers members in Stockton more than 50 specialties, programs, and services as part of its integrated health care approach. Kaiser, which opened its first medical office in the city in 1984, also contracts with inpatient medical centers and community health care providers to serve its members in the region.

Kaiser has smaller medical offices in outlying communities and is a major employer in the area. In the fall of 2008, Kaiser added a key facility to its Central Valley region with its Modesto Medical Center, located about 30 miles southeast of Stockton. It is the first major hospital built in the region in almost four decades. Kaiser also participates in local community health efforts and awards grants for public health care.

Sutter Gould Medical Foundation, a health care group formed in 1986, has three care centers in Stockton, including a three-story, 70,000-square-foot medical plaza housing physicians in primary care, obstetrics and gynecology, and endocrinology. The plaza also has an imaging center and clinical laboratory services.

Among medical specialty groups, Stockton Cardiology Medical Group (SCMG) has been at the forefront of cardiac care for 56 years. The original partners brought many advances to Stockton, including the first heart catheter laboratory in conjunction with the first coronary care unit, CPR protocols and education, and the first in-office nuclear medicine laboratory in northern California. The doctors have privileges at both St. Joseph's Medical Center and Dameron Hospital in Stockton. The group also has offices and hospital affiliations in Manteca, Tracy, and San Andreas.

Delta Health Care, one of Stockton's many free or low-cost health clinics, offers services and information to a wide range of local residents. The center has a multicultural staff that reflects Stockton's diversity, with health care workers who can speak or translate in English, Spanish, and many Southeast Asian languages. The center focuses on reproductive health, health education, nutrition training, and teen outreach.

For patients who need home health care, Gentiva Health Services, a leading national provider, provides nursing, wound care, rehabilitation, and other services to Stockton residents. To help senior citizens be steadier on their feet and avoid falls, Gentiva's Safe Strides program evaluates and treats balance problems and assesses the home environment.

In addition to medical care, Stockton has many other ways to keep its citizens healthy and happy. Oak Park Senior Citizens Center has exercise classes, dancing and singing groups, and sports leagues. Stockton has several senior residential communities and dozens of child-care centers tailored to meet each individual family's needs.

Stockton is not a big city, but it has many of the educational and health care options one would expect to find in larger metropolitan areas. This bodes well for residents as well as for professionals in these fields and the businesses that serve them.

CHAPTER FOUR

ENABLING PROSPERITY

Financial, Professional, and Business Services

From its historic beginnings as a supply stop for miners and a center of prosperous agricultural and shipping enterprises, Stockton has always been a business and commercial hub. While pioneers and farmers tilled the land and established homesteads, shops began to dot the landscape as entrepreneurs built businesses from the rich valley ground up. That pioneer spirit—the hard work and vision, the innovation and adaptability—is reflected today in Stockton's array of professional and business services. As the city continues to widen its economic base from its strong agricultural moorings, more professional and financial businesses open and expand in Stockton. From banks and insurance agencies to architects, developers, and information technology services, Stockton is rich in its ability to envision, safeguard, create, and grow.

Professional and business service providers are increasingly taking advantage of Stockton's strategic location between the state's capital and the San Francisco Bay area, along with the area's affordable land and commercial prosperity. Dreams come in all shapes and sizes, and Stockton's financial and professional businesses are there to encourage and protect those dreams.

Banking Choices

Banks, always an integral part of Stockton's commercial scene, are flourishing, thanks to the city's steady growth. Today, customers have a multitude of banks with dozens of branches to choose from in Stockton. From small independent banks to larger, more diversified financial institutions, Stockton has just the right fit for every business's needs.

Bank of Stockton, a 141-year tradition in the city, has been growing with Stockton since the institution's founding as Stockton Savings and Loan in 1867. The bank, founded by 29 self-made businessmen, opened its doors in the depressed economic times following the Civil War. In the early 1900s, the bank built the city's first skyscraper, an eight-story building. Today, the bank has 16 branches in five counties, is approaching $2 billion in assets, and has branched out to include commerce banks in Modesto, Turlock, and Elk Grove.

Farmers and Merchants Bank of Central California, a full-service community bank headquartered in Lodi, has been offering financial services to Central Valley residents and businesses since 1916. Today, it has 23 locations in the community.

In 1965, the Berberian family, Central Valley business people for more than 50 years, opened the Bank of Agriculture and Commerce. The bank, headquartered in Stockton, now has locations in eight communities, including its ECC Bank division serving east Contra Costa County. The bank specializes in services to local professionals.

In 1999, after several mergers and acquisitions in the banking industry, local investors felt Stockton was ripe for a smaller, local bank, and Community Bank of San Joaquin was launched. Today, the full-service community bank has almost $150 million in assets and two branches.

Guaranty Bank, based in Texas, showed its commitment to Stockton with its new 15,000-square-foot building downtown. In addition to the downtown location, which houses the bank's regional office for statewide operations, the bank has four branches in Stockton.

Bank of the West, which serves nearly four million households in 19 states, has eight branches in Stockton, while Bank of America has five branches in the area. Wells Fargo, which has thousands of branches in 23 states, has four locations in Stockton. Also serving Stockton are many credit unions, including Financial Center Credit Union, with nearly 35,000 members. Central State Credit Union, founded in 1936 for state employees in the region, is now a community credit union with more than 23,000 members.

Expert Professionals

Stockton has an array of legal expertise to serve its complex business, government, and personal needs. One of the most noteworthy firms is Neumiller & Beardslee, which dates back to 1903 and is part of the history of the area. The firm was there at the creation of the Caterpillar Tractor Company, and it was involved in major public works projects such as the New Melones Dam, completed in 1979. The firm represents public entities, corporations, and developers as well as individuals. More than 24 attorneys specialize in many areas of practice, from business law to water rights.

For accounting expertise, the city has a number of certified public accountants (CPAs). One firm with a scope of services, from Internet commerce to fraud prevention to retirement planning, is Iacopi, Lenz & Company. Founded in 1978, the firm has 17 CPAs who provide personalized service to individuals and businesses.

Stockton also has many choices when it comes to insurance to protect businesses and residents. Dozens of agencies operate in the area, from smaller independent offices to larger, nationally branded companies, insuring everything from life to property, home titles, businesses, and automobiles. Delta Health Systems, a third-party health insurance administrator with clients nationwide, is based in Stockton.

Designing and Building

With at least 20 architects making their home in Stockton, there is no trouble finding a professional to bring vision and art to life. Stockton has a diverse range of planners and architects to handle everything from the most basic home design or remodel to more complicated assignments, such as government institutions, housing communities, and commercial and industrial projects. Many Stockton architects have benefited from a building boom in the last several years, designing new schools, churches, and whole neighborhoods of homes and office buildings in northern California.

LDA Partners in Stockton is representative of the caliber of work done by local architects. Founded in 1979 by Brent Lesovsky and joined the next year by partner Michael Donaldson, the firm started by concentrating on designs for the residential and health care sectors, but has since diversified to community, commercial, office, and historic renovation projects. The company designed the five-story, 150,000-square-foot complex housing the corporate offices of the A. G. Spanos Companies in Stockton, the 18,000-square-foot Van Buskirk Community Center, a 10,000-square-foot student fitness center addition at the University of the Pacific, and the Wine and Roses Inn and Spa and the adjacent Wine and Visitors Center, both in Lodi. Another local firm, Lee-Jagoe Architecture, offers land planning services and designs for custom homes, retail centers, offices, and even golf course communities.

This page, left: The Bob Hope Theatre, with renovation led by WMB Architects; this page, right: Dean DeCarli Waterfront Square, an award-winning design by Derivi Construction and Architecture. Opposite page: Podesto Impact Teen Center designed by LDA Partners.

Recent redevelopment efforts in the downtown area also have spurred a flurry of historic restoration and construction projects for local architects, such as the Bob Hope Theatre, renovated by WMB Architects, and Dean DeCarli Waterfront Square at Stockton's historic channel, an award-winning design by Derivi Construction and Architecture.

Major Developers

Without developers, of course, none of the designs could become reality. Stockton's development community has fueled growth for generations, in Stockton, in northern California, and even nationwide. One of the largest and best-known developers to shape neighborhoods and business centers is the nationally recognized A. G. Spanos Companies. Founded in Stockton in 1960 by Alex Spanos, the builder-developer has completed more than 400 developments in California and 21 other states. These include more than 120,000 apartment units, more than two million square feet of office space, master-planned communities, and mixed-use developments. The Spanos communities feature upscale amenities, spacious floor plans, and landscaped grounds.

This page, left: Brookside, a Grupe Company development; this page, right: The award-winning Cheval apartment complex in Houston by the A. G. Spanos Companies. Opposite page: Information technology (IT) services available in Stockton.

The Grupe Company, founded in 1966, has designed and built master-planned communities and more than 50,000 homes in 35 cities. Grupe's plans encourage social interaction, including homes with front porches, pedestrian-friendly sidewalks, and plenty of parks and gathering areas. Stockton's development community also includes smaller firms that do custom homes, offices, and retail projects.

Technology Services

Information technology services are taking off in Stockton, as many high-tech companies transplant from the San Francisco Bay area, and new technology consulting and telecommunications firms start up in the city. In addition to larger regional and national companies, Stockton area entrepreneurs have launched enterprises providing phone and Internet services and support. These businesses are attracted to Stockton by its proximity to the Silicon Valley and the Bay Area, its less expensive and abundant land, and a better quality of life for employees. They also are finding customers in the booming commercial and retail environment.

Technology service companies showcase some of the region's most innovative spirits, like Steve Fetzer, who in 1998 started his own telephone company, CCT Online, based in Lodi. The homegrown company offers business and residential customers local dial-tone phone service for local and long-distance use, broadband and dial-up Internet, Web design, hosting, and e-mail, all typically at a cheaper price and with localized customer care. CCT has shown growth every year since its founding. Companies like McDaniel Analysis and Research, founded in Stockton in 2000, also offer customers technology consulting, including data management, security, and Web and software services.

Stockton has the scope of business and professional services that a growing economy needs. The availability of financing, professional services, and technology will give businesses the competitive edge necessary to maximize profits while sustaining growth.

This page: A pumpkin patch, a fall favorite in the Stockton area.
Opposite page: Working a field of alfalfa, an important crop in
fertile San Joaquin County.

CHAPTER FIVE

TREASURES FROM THE EARTH
Agriculture and Viniculture

Soon after the Gold Rush subsided in northern California, pioneers found another treasure in the low-lying volcanic soils of the Stockton area: farming. Today, Stockton relies on its historic roots in agriculture not only for jobs and open space, but also as a solid foundation for the region's economic base, including value-added farm products and spin-off industries. In fact, economists say every dollar made in agriculture in the Stockton area rolls over seven times in the economy.

An Agricultural Giant

San Joaquin County, the fifth-largest area in agricultural production in California, produces more than $2 billion worth of agricultural commodities a year. The economic impact of farming ripples into packing sheds, transportation industries, pest control businesses, veterinarian supplies and services, fertilizer, and scientific research and technology companies. The county has 143 trading partners worldwide, with its farm products exported to countries from Afghanistan to Zimbabwe. The region is a leader in sustainable agriculture, including use of environmentally friendly pest control. "You pick" farms, pumpkin patches, corn mazes, and the ever-increasing number of wineries opening to the public are driving a growing agricultural tourism trend, showcasing agriculture's importance in the economy and in the community's quality of life.

Milk is typically the largest cash commodity of the area, with the county's dairies pulling in more than $466 million in 2007. Grapes constitute a large force in the economy of the Stockton area, with table and wine grapes grossing close to $217 million in 2007. Tomatoes, almonds, and walnuts are also top commodities in terms of value, accounting for hundreds of millions of dollars in sales.

Celebrating Asparagus

The area's crop of asparagus, known as the "queen of vegetables," is the guest of honor at the annual Stockton Asparagus Festival, a three-day spring rite celebrating the elegance and versatility of the green spear. Stockton's asparagus crop, valued at around $32 million annually, is one of the largest in the world, and festival volunteers cook thousands of pounds of deep-fried asparagus. The festival, in its 23rd year in 2008, featured 70 food vendors, many of them asparagus-related, a wine-and-beer pavilion, and cooking demonstrations by celebrity chefs.

The county is the state's top producer of pumpkins, cherries, asparagus, beans, feed corn, apples, English walnuts, and safflower. It is also in the top five for statewide production for 12 other commodities. One crop with high economic potential is blueberries, which will increase in sales as consumers realize the berry's health benefits. The county's acreage of blueberries increased ninefold in the past five years, reaching a value approximating $8.4 million and vaulting San Joaquin County to one of the state's leaders in the blueberry market.

Cherries are a more than $201 million crop in the area, and the short harvest and packing season at the end of May causes a flurry of picking and packing in the picturesque orchards northeast of Stockton. Meanwhile apples, currently a $38 million crop, are gaining a foothold, as growers plant new orchards of varieties popular with consumers: Fuji, Royal Gala, and Pink Lady.

On the Wine Trail

While harvested acreage in San Joaquin County fluctuates slightly, the area's land in farm production has hovered at 75 percent to 80 percent in the last decade. The most exciting spike in acreage has been the new plantings of wine grape varieties, as the Stockton and Lodi regions emerged as a major grape-growing appellation in the past 20 years. The area has grown fresh table grapes for worldwide consumption and provided grapes to Napa and Sonoma's wine-making operations for more than a century, but now is coming into its own, growing specific varieties, with many vineyards crushing and bottling on site and opening tasting rooms to a blossoming tourist trade. Many of the county's zinfandel vines planted in the 1800s survived both Prohibition and the planting booms of other varieties in the 1970s and 1980s, and they have been resuscitated as the centerpiece of the industry today.

Delicato Winery, with its award-winning wines and worldwide distribution, is head-quartered in Manteca, just miles south of Stockton. Lodi's Woodbridge community is home to a large Robert Mondavi winery and tasting room and almost 50 other boutique wineries, 34 of which have tasting rooms on the Lodi Wine Trail.

At many family-owned wineries, visitors may taste wine with the vineyard owner, who could very well be a fifth-generation wine-grape grower from the region. In nearby Lockeford, Vino Piazza houses eight independent wineries in a refurbished 1946 winery and distillery, featuring dozens of wines for tasting in a Tuscan-style plaza.

This page: Emerald Trail Mix, part of Diamond Foods of Stockton, a leading processor and marketer of nuts. Opposite page: Sliced apples for packing and shipping by air at Farmington Fresh.

Foods for the World

Agriculture is a jumping-off place for many other innovative industries, as local entrepreneurs constantly think of ways to create new markets and expand and refine existing ones for commodities. Fresh fruit and vegetable packing sheds and nut processing and distribution are good examples of value-added farm products creating jobs and markets in the Stockton area. The countryside around Stockton is dotted with apple, cherry, asparagus, tomato, and pear sheds buzzing with activity during harvest time.

Farmington Fresh, located in south Stockton, is one of the country's premier grower/packer/shippers of fresh fruits, and the only produce shipper in the world operated out of a major airport. The company ships cherries and whole and sliced apples from Stockton Metropolitan Airport, allowing easy movement of products to market.

Diamond Foods, headquartered in Stockton, is a leading processor and marketer of nuts, both for ingredients and snacking. It sells a line of walnuts, pine nuts, pecans, peanuts, and almonds, among other products. Walnuts from local orchards are a $133 million crop, and Diamond has holdings throughout the world. The company's products are sold in more than 60,000 retail locations in the United States, and in more than 100 countries worldwide. Diamond is the nation's leading exporter of walnuts to Europe and the Pacific Rim.

Ace Tomato Company in Manteca ships two million cartons of fresh tomatoes every year, packed in one of the most technically advanced plants in the western United States, and distributed domestically and internationally. Ace is part of the Lagorio Family of Companies that also produces a variety of other crops, from apples and asparagus to beans. The enterprise includes a packing company and an international marketing company.

In another hometown success story, Dean Cortopassi, a young man from an Italian immigrant family, started farming 60 acres in 1960 and nursed it into a 10,000-acre diversified farming operation. Today, his San Tomo Group operates California food processing and marketing companies. He is also involved with family-owned Corto Olive, an olive-oil plant in Lodi now its third harvest season. Corto's olive farming involves high-density planting and advanced mechanical harvesting in which the olives never touch the ground.

This page, left: Local olive oil; this page, right: Holt of California for Caterpillar tractors and more. Opposite page, left: One of the two million cartons of Ace Tomatoes shipped each year; opposite page, right: Corn destined for many uses at Corn Products International.

Refined for Many Uses

At the Corn Products International plant in Stockton, corn grown locally and in the Midwest is refined into sweeteners and starches used for food manufacturing, animal feed, paper, and textiles. Powering the Corn Products plant is the adjacent cogeneration facility, a coal-fired plant that makes electricity and steam. Air Products and Chemicals operates and co-owns the power facility.

Tilling, Treating, and Seeding the Land

To produce this agricultural bounty, growers need the right equipment and supplies. For large machinery, Holt of California provides Caterpillar-manufactured equipment to a 16-county region. The Illinois-based Caterpillar brand, the leader in track-type earthmoving and agricultural equipment, traces its origin to Stockton, where Benjamin Holt invented the track-type tractor in 1904. Through the Stockton and other dealerships, Holt of California continues to serve the agricultural, construction, material handling, and other industries of the region.

This page: Irrigated tomato plants near Stockton. Opposite page: A representative from J. R. Simplot's Grower Solutions advising a farmer about the soil's fertilizer needs,

For everything from fertilizer to seed, the J. R. Simplot Company, a global agribusiness, has a presence in San Joaquin County. In Lathrop, south of Stockton, the company produces fertilizer, which is sold in bulk or in 50-pound bags. In nearby French Camp, it has a bulk fertilizer distribution center. At the Port of Stockton, Simplot imports nitrogen products through a terminal owned by the California Ammonia Company (CALAMCO), a growers' cooperative in which Simplot is a major shareholder. North of Stockton, in Lodi, Simplot's Grower Solutions farm service center offers agronomic expertise, equipment, technology, and products.

Agriculture remains king in San Joaquin County. By adapting to changing markets and employing modern technology, agricultural businesses in the Stockton area have grown mouthwatering foods for the country and the world, contributed to many aspects of agribusiness, created thousands of jobs, and reaped billions of dollars for the local economy.

CHAPTER SIX

BY LAND, WATER, AND AIR
Transportation and Logistics

Stockton is one of an archipelago of jewels on a strand weaving through California's Central Valley, connected to statewide, national, and global urban markets through strong transportation networks. Because of its central location in the heart of California and a vibrant transportation system, Stockton is easy to get to from just about anywhere in the state. San Joaquin County is a hub of northern California manufacturing and distribution, and new and growing businesses run on the transportation veins pulsing through the Stockton region, by land, water, and air.

Highway Connections

Stockton is nurtured by a patchwork of roadways for commuters, tourists, and freight delivery. Two primary north-south arteries serve the city: Interstate 5 is a major West Coast route for moving freight from Mexico to Canada, while California Highway 99 is a main route linking cities in California's Central Valley. The Stockton Crosstown Freeway (California Highway 4) and California Highway 120 join these arteries, adding to the network. Just minutes away, Interstate 205 is a connector between Interstate 5 on the east and Interstate 580 on the west.

From Interstate 205, Interstate 580 runs west and north toward Oakland and the San Francisco Bay area, about 80 miles away. Meanwhile, to the north, Interstate 80, a major U.S. roadway, runs from San Francisco through Sacramento, Reno, Nevada, and hubs eastward, terminating in New Jersey. Major trucking companies and independent contract carriers in the San Joaquin County area number in the hundreds, much of that business spurred by the manufacturing and farming operations in and around Stockton.

In summer and fall, Stockton's roadways are alive with the bustle of agricultural trucking, from loads of tomatoes and onions to fruit concentrate and wine grapes. Cherokee Freight Lines is an example of a small trucking operation that capitalized on Stockton's agribusiness economy to catapult it to success. Gary Scannavino started the trucking line in 1966, building on a Stockton business that his father started with one truck in 1945. The line started out specializing in transporting winery-related products and expanded into food grade commodities shipped to some of the largest companies in the nation, and now includes kosher-certified hauling and special tanks for granulated sugar.

Linked by Rail

Stockton's unique location puts it at a crossroads for major railways. Railroads, the lifeline of California farmers and entrepreneurs of yesteryear, have again taken a leading role in connecting Stockton to the rest of the nation. Two railways, the Burlington Northern Santa Fe (BNSF) and the Union Pacific (UP), figure largely in the city's transportation scenario. Both railways have intermodal facilities in Stockton to transfer cargo containers that are transported by different modes, including rail, truck, and ship. In this way, the cargo does not need to be handled, improving security, reducing loss and damage, and saving costs over traditional freight trucking, especially for export products. The BNSF intermodal center in southeast Stockton, completed in 2001, lifts an average of more than 600 specially designed freight-train containers a day. The UP intermodal facility in Stockton lifts an average of 200 to 250 containers a day.

This page, left: Passengers at the Amtrak station in Stockton; this page, right: San Joaquin Regional Transit District (RTD) buses at the Downtown Transit Center (DTC), including one bus equipped with hybrid technology. Opposite page: The Altamont Commuter Express (ACE) train that carries passengers to and from San Jose.

Stockton commuters also have an array of choices for staying on track. Amtrak's San Joaquins route runs a passenger train several times a day through the heartland of the Central Valley, from the San Francisco Bay area and Sacramento to Bakersfield, making stops in Stockton. The train also regularly whisks people away to Merced, where they board a waiting bus and travel to scenic Yosemite National Park. Other connections include the Six Flags Amusement Park in Vallejo, connecting in Martinez, or riders can link up to other routes and travel to popular destinations such as Las Vegas, Palm Springs, Santa Barbara, and Los Angeles. A regional rail service, Altamont Commuter Express (ACE), carries passengers from Stockton to San Jose through the Altamont Pass. The service runs multiple trains daily in each direction, making 10 stops along its 86-mile route on Union Pacific rails.

Getting Around the County

Buses from the San Joaquin Regional Transit District (RTD) carry passengers throughout area cities and the county, with connections beyond. The transit district logged nearly four million trips in 2007. Routes connect Stockton, Lodi, Tracy, Manteca, Ripon, Lathrop, and other parts of the county. From the new Downtown Transit Center (DTC) in Stockton, riders can link to almost all RTD bus routes. For getting around the central city, the Downtown Trolley is quick and fun. The RTD fleet includes hybrid buses.

Major Inland Port

Stockton is fortunate to have one of the nation's few major inland deepwater channel ports. The Port of Stockton, a 2,000-acre transportation center set on the banks of the San Joaquin River, has 15,000 lineal feet of docks and 15 vessel berths. The complex also has 1.1 million square feet of transit sheds near the docks and 7.7 million square feet of warehouse operations. The site has direct ship-to-rail service and served by the BNSF and UP railroads.

The port has deep-rooted historic connections to Stockton's navigable waterways. The meandering channels of the San Joaquin River Delta were fished and navigated by Native Americans for centuries. Before and during the California Gold Rush, Stockton was a natural landing for riverboats. After the Gold Rush, farmers continued to use the waterfront to ship and receive goods from all over the world for the remainder of the 19th century and into the 20th.

In 1933 a project was completed to modernize the riverfront and to dredge the channel, roughly 75 nautical miles of waterways, to San Francisco Bay, creating the Stockton Deepwater Ship Channel. The Port of Stockton opened that year, positioned for commercial growth as it could serve larger, heavier vessels. These improvements also led to the creation of a U.S. naval supply base, Rough and Ready Island, next to the port. The base was decommissioned in 1995 and later taken over by the port for commercial shipping. By 2008, as the port celebrated 75 years in operation, the facility was handling more than seven million tons of cargo a year. Its top export was bagged California rice. Three 30-ton bridge cranes at the port, along with floating and mobile truck cranes, load and unload tons of goods, including steel, coal, lumber, and liquid and dry bulk materials. Two bulk loading towers also load materials for export.

The port is home base for major distribution and warehousing operations. In recognition of Stockton's strategic location and rising importance as a distribution hub, Lowe's, the world's second-largest home improvement retailer, opened its flatbed distribution center on 23 acres at the port in 2007. The $16 million, 240,000-square-foot plant receives rail and truck shipments of building materials and home improvement goods, then loads the products onto flatbed trucks for distribution to more than 40 retail stores in northern California, Nevada, and Oregon. The center is one of 13 nationwide for Lowe's.

Ferguson Enterprises, a nationwide distributor of plumbing fixtures, pipe, sprinklers, and air-conditioning and heating parts based in Virginia, announced plans in 2006 for a major distribution center at Rough and Ready Island. The 650,000-square-foot distribution facility sits on 58 acres and would create up to 250 jobs. Sygma, a subsidiary of Sysco Corp., also has one of 17 distribution centers nationwide in Stockton. Sygma provides restaurant supplies from fresh beef and vegetables to cleaning supplies and utensils to more than 12,800 restaurants nationwide.

A Distribution Nucleus

Stockton offers distribution and warehousing system advantages beyond the port. Crown Bolt moved into a new 200,000-square-foot building in a south Stockton industrial park in 2002. The company supplies the hardware and home center industry, including importing, packaging, and distributing fasteners and other hardware. The company wanted to establish a western hub, and Stockton, with access to two freeways, provided a good location. Other companies with distribution centers in Stockton include Dollar Tree and Cost Plus World Market.

To top it off, Stockton has the Dorfman Pacific hat company, which has its corporate headquarters and distribution center in a 275,000-square-foot facility near the airport. The company prides itself on being one of the largest full-line, in-stock headware and handbag companies in the world.

Access by Air

For those wanting to wing it, Stockton is also accessible by air. The city is served by Stockton Metropolitan Airport, just southeast of Stockton's central business district. It is a lively hub for the shipping of manufacturing products and agricultural goods, including export shipments of local farm products. Designated by the U.S. Department of Commerce as a foreign trade zone, it is a special customs area that offers reduced export duties and fewer customs restrictions. Passenger flights to Las Vegas are available through Allegiant Air, and talks are in progress for bringing expanded passenger lines.

Stockton truly is a crossroads city, site of the convergence of various modes of transportation, and a modern transit center for many products and commodities. By making transportation and distribution more efficient, a Stockton location provides an economic advantage for businesses.

PART TWO
SUCCESS STORIES:
PROFILES OF COMPANIES AND ORGANIZATIONS

PROFILES OF COMPANIES AND ORGANIZATIONS
Agribusiness and Consumer Goods

J. R. Simplot Company

A world leader in agribusiness, the J. R. Simplot Company delivers high quality food products to customers in the foodservice industry around the globe. This company is also a major supplier of industrial and agricultural products, cattle feed and beef, and turf and horticultural products.

Above: Simplot Grower Solutions employees and other company representatives assist farmers with many aspects of their businesses. J. R. Simplot Company employs about 20 people at its Grower Solutions operations in San Joaquin County, which include a retail farm service center in Lodi and an administrative office in Stockton.

The J. R. Simplot Company, based in Boise, Idaho, is a global agribusiness corporation serving markets in the United States, Canada, Europe, Mexico, Australia, Japan, China, and the Pacific Rim.

Founded in 1923, Simplot is ranked by *Forbes* magazine as one of the largest privately owned companies in the nation. With more than $3.5 billion in annual revenue, Simplot businesses span the production and distribution of agricultural fertilizers, food processing, farming, horticulture, and ranching.

Its mission statement, "Bringing Earth's Resources to Life," embodies the company's reason for being in business.

Two Simplot mines in Idaho and Utah provide the large quantities of phosphate ore needed to produce many of the company's fertilizer products.

At its manufacturing plants in Lathrop and Helm, California; Pocatello, Idaho; and Rock Springs, Wyoming, Simplot annually produces several million tons of dry and liquid fertilizers.

The Lathrop plant sells fertilizer in bulk or in 50-pound bags. Lathrop's professional turf and ornamental products are sold under the BEST and APEX brands, and used mainly by golf courses, landscapers, and commercial nurseries in the western United States and other countries, primarily in the Pacific Rim. The Lathrop facility also manufactures ammonium sulfate, sulfuric acid, and feed-grade phosphate, which is a nutritional supplement for livestock and poultry. The plant employs about 150 people.

Simplot's Helm plant makes nitrogen-based solutions for agricultural and industrial use and distributes dry products made at other Simplot plants. The Helm facility employs 36 people.

Simplot also has bulk fertilizer distribution centers at French Camp and El Centro, California, which employ four and five people, respectively.

Simplot complements its U.S. fertilizer manufacturing capabilities with imported nitrogen products routed through its storage and distribution terminals at Point Comfort, Texas, and Portland,

Oregon, and a Stockton terminal owned by California Ammonia Company (CALAMCO), a growers cooperative in which Simplot is a major shareholder.

The CALAMCO facility has capacity for about 40,000 tons of anhydrous ammonia and 40,000 tons of liquid urea ammonium nitrate.

While Simplot's agricultural fertilizers help promote crop growth, the company also plays a significant role in developing healthy, vibrant turf for a variety of uses. Simplot is a major global supplier through its Jacklin Seed and Simplot Partners businesses to the turfgrass and horticulture industries, with distribution in North America, South America, Europe, and Asia.

The Simplot Grower Solutions network of 80 farm service centers provides a

vital link in the food chain by offering the best in equipment, technology, products, and agronomic expertise to farmers in the West and the Midwest. The Lodi unit in San Joaquin County is one of 10 in California. The Lodi operation employs 12 people.

After growers harvest their crops, another important part of the company comes into play. Simplot plants located in the United States, Canada, Mexico, Australia, and China process frozen potato items, avocado products, and other foods into a wide variety of value-added offerings.

Worldwide, Simplot is a leader in the potato processing business, annually turning out more than three billion pounds of frozen french fries and other potato products for foodservice distributors, quick-service and full-service restaurants, and many other customers.

Simplot farms grow some of the potatoes used in the company's U.S. plants, however, most come from more than 200 independent growers who work nearly 100,000 acres of crop land.

The company's state-of-the-industry processing plant at Portage la Prairie, Manitoba, produces frozen potato products for clients in the eastern and midwestern United States. The Beijing potato plant turns out french fries for quick-service restaurants and other clients in China, and Simplot operates several vegetable plants in Mexico. Simplot food plants in Australia serve retail, foodservice, and export customers.

Simplot is the West's largest beef cattle producer and the only firm in the top 10 nationwide for both cow-calf production and feedlot cattle capacity.

Simplot ranches in four western states supply the majority of incoming stock for its feedlots in Idaho and Washington, while independent ranchers annually fill some of the need for feeder cattle.

Simplot provides additional information about the company and its activities on its Web site (www.simplot.com).

In addition to understanding the ingredients of building a successful business, Simplot is keenly aware of its ecological responsibilities. The company's electrical cogeneration unit at its Lathrop plant and participation in Green Team San Joaquin through the Greater Stockton Chamber of Commerce are examples of this commitment to the environment.

The company also supports a variety of school and civic activities in many communities that are home to its plants, offices, and other facilities.

Although much has changed since J. R. Simplot started his first produce company in 1929, the company's principles are the same today as they were then: "Keep your rig in the best possible shape, hire good people, and give honest value for a fair price."

Above left: Simplot fertilizer manufacturing plants at Lathrop, California; Pocatello, Idaho; and Rock Springs, Wyoming, operate cogeneration equipment that produces electricity for internal use and sale to local utility companies. Above right: The Simplot fertilizer manufacturing plant at Lathrop produces bagged and bulk products for a wide variety of customers. The plant employs approximately 150 people.

Ace Tomato Co., Inc.

Part of a large family of companies with a long history in the San Joaquin Valley, this tomato grower emphasizes food safety and high quality in every step of its operations. It offers a wide assortment of field-grown tomato products to customers throughout North America and Asia.

Ace Tomato Co., Inc.'s history began in 1967. At the time, George B. Lagorio, the son of Italian farmers who had immigrated to the San Joaquin Valley, was one of the company's growers. His own farming career had begun in 1945, when he purchased 30 acres of land from his parents. He quickly expanded his 30 acres to 1,400 acres and was producing a variety of crops, including tomatoes, sugar beets, alfalfa, and barley. By the mid 1970s, Lagorio had acquired full ownership of Ace Tomato and had moved the company to its present location near Stockton in Manteca.

A Family of Companies

Today Ace Tomato is part of the Lagorio Family of Companies, which comprises five businesses: Ace Tomato Co., Inc., Delta Pre-Pack Company Inc., Lagorio Farming Company, Ace International Marketing, and Lagorio Leasing. Delta Pre-Pack Company Inc. provides a year-round supply of tomatoes by working with growing partners in both Florida and Mexico to supplement tomatoes it grows in the summer in San Joaquin County. Lagorio Farming produces a variety of crops including walnuts, wine grapes, and cherries, some of which it pioneered in the region. Today this company continues that tradition. Ace International Marketing is a central marketing and sales service for all Lagorio companies. Lagorio Leasing Company manages farm equipment used throughout the companies. Together the Lagorio Family of Companies is an industry leader in growing, packing, and shipping high quality fruits and vegetables.

The companies' farms are located on 10,000 acres in the fertile San Joaquin Valley, in California's Central Valley. The 21-acre Manteca location includes packing warehouses, temperature-controlled storage rooms, shipping facilities, and a corporate office building. From Manteca, Ace Tomato ships millions of cartons of tomatoes to clients throughout North America and Asia.

The Lagorio family plays a major role in the companies' leadership today. George Lagorio's daughter is CEO of the Lagorio Family of Companies. Her husband and sons are also involved in the family businesses. The Lagorio family motto is "pride in every phase of our operation."

A Tradition of Quality

Like the other members of the Lagorio Family of Companies, Ace Tomato has a long-standing tradition of offering a variety of high quality products and flexible packaging options while adhering to industry-leading food safety standards and delivering outstanding service. Ace Tomato products include vine-ripened, grape, Roma, and mature green tomatoes.

To ensure high quality products, Ace Tomato takes measures throughout the farming process to establish quality. It takes into account soil, weather, and season to select the best seeds, which are germinated in greenhouses. As the

seedlings grow, Ace Tomato selects only the hardiest plants to be placed in its fields.

After harvest, Ace Tomato is able to deliver tomatoes that are ready for market when they reach the warehouse or are ripened and packed to suit particular customers' specifications.

Safety, the First Consideration

At Ace Tomato, the company takes a "farm-to-fork" approach when it comes to food safety. Its goal is to provide the highest quality and safest vegetables possible—and safety begins on the farm.

Trace-back is a vital component of Ace Tomato's food-safety protocols and ensures that the company has a record of where its product was harvested, packed, and shipped. The company's trace-back system provides its customers with confidence in knowing where their product has been at every step in the supply chain.

Through the company's rigorous food-safety protocols and procedures, it is able to provide its customers and consumers with not only the best quality products but also products that are wholesome, nutritious, and safe.

Philanthropic Community Support

Demonstrating a tradition of philanthropy, the Lagorio family is committed to supporting the Stockton community. To that end, it has established the Janssen/Lagorio Family Foundation. Important causes supported by this organization include medical research, education, and community interests.

Throughout its long history, Ace Tomato has maintained its traditions of innovation, philanthropy, and pride in its products. Along with the other Lagorio companies, it will continue to build on the principles of year-round supply, variety of product offerings, flexible packaging options, and high food-safety standards to provide outstanding service and high quality products.

Above left: Ace Tomato is located near Manteca, California, in the center of the San Joaquin Valley. Above right: The tomatoes produced in Manteca are grown during the summer. Left: The company's tomatoes are harvested when they are mature green and can be ripened to customer specifications in the company's 135,000-carton capacity degreening rooms.

Corn Products International, Inc.

This plant in Stockton, part of one of the world's largest corn refining and ingredient companies, converts corn into sweeteners and starches for beverages, baking, candy, canning, corrugation, and other important industries and also supplies corn gluten feed and meal to cattle and poultry producers in the San Joaquin Valley.

Above left: Corn Products International, Inc.'s Stockton plant uses several local transportation companies to haul finished products to local markets in the San Joaquin Valley. Here, a local trucker exits the Stockton plant with a load of high fructose corn syrup. In the background are the steep tanks used to soften the corn prior to the grinding operation. Above right: Although corn is purchased locally during harvest time in the San Joaquin Valley and processed at the Corn Products plant, due to the large quantity of corn required by the process, much of the corn is purchased in the Midwest and delivered by rail to the plant. Here, Matt Myrick, a field operator, unloads corn from a railcar.

Soft drinks, cereals, baked goods, canned foods, corrugated boxes, animal feeds—these are products that Stockton-area residents use every day. And they are made possible by ingredients made by Corn Products International, Inc. and its Stockton plant.

Headquartered in the Chicago suburb of Westchester, Illinois, Corn Products International is one of the world's leading producers of corn starches, sweeteners, and syrups. Founded more than 100 years ago, its ingredients are the building blocks of some of the world's most common and important products, from foods and beverages to pharmaceuticals, intravenous (IV) solutions, pet foods, animal feeds, paper, and textiles.

Corn Products' Stockton plant is an important part of the company's North American business. It converts one of America's most versatile and abundant crops—corn—into sweeteners and industrial starches that are used by the beverage, baking, canning, candy, and corrugated industries.

The facility also produces corn gluten feed and meal for producers of beef, dairy products, and poultry in the San Joaquin Valley.

Since opening its doors in Stockton in 1981, Corn Products has become a vital part of the region's business community. Its location near Interstate 5 and Highway 99 provides easy access for both suppliers and customers. The plant employs area residents in self-directed, round-the-clock shifts in an environment that stresses employee safety above everything else. On the other side of the plant's fence, Air Products and Chemicals, Inc. (the Stockton Cogeneration Company) operates an environmentally compliant, coal-fired cogeneration facility that provides the steam and electricity that powers the Corn Products plant. This arrangement is a 20-year-old partnership that has paid dividends not only for the two companies but also for California consumers, since Stockton Cogeneration supplies its excess power to the state's electric grid.

Corn Products International is an active and caring corporate neighbor. The Stockton plant is a member of the California Chamber of Commerce, the Greater Stockton Chamber of Commerce, the Business Council of San Joaquin County, and the San Joaquin Safety Council. It contributes directly to neighboring schools to assist with class trips and technology improvements and is a Platinum-level donor to United Way of San Joaquin County in Stockton.

As a longtime business partner and industry leader that provides vital ingredients for some of the world's most important products, Corn Products International's Stockton facility plays a key part in commerce in the San Joaquin Valley.

PROFILES OF COMPANIES AND ORGANIZATIONS
Community Banking

Bank of Stockton

For more than 141 years, this financial institution has served the Gold Rush town of Stockton with the highest standards for quality banking products, technological innovation, and customer satisfaction. Its history is one of strength, service, and commitment to generations of satisfied customers.

Right: The ribbon-cutting ceremony for the grand opening of the Bank of Stockton's headquarters at 301 East Miner Avenue took place on March 10, 1960. Bill Murphy, then California Superintendent of Banks, cuts the ribbon with the assistance of Robert M. Eberhardt's daughters Bonnie and Mary Elizabeth Eberhardt. Robert M. Eberhardt would later succeed his father, R. L. Eberhardt, as president of the Bank of Stockton.

Seeking financial stability just two years after the Civil War, 29 visionary businessmen in Stockton pledged $100,000 in gold coins to provide a safe and stable place for people's money during a most tumultuous time. The bank filed its certificate of incorporation on August 12, 1867, and opened its doors for business a few weeks later. Ever since, the Bank of Stockton has been a cornerstone of tradition, strength, and service.

The bank's original officers and stockholders were prominent landowners and self-made businessmen. They were also active members of the community. The bank's first president, J. M. Kelsey, was the San Joaquin County treasurer and tax collector. The bank's first cashier, James Littlehale, was the Stockton city treasurer. And Andrew W. Simpson, one of the bank's vice presidents for 54 years, was also a member of the Weber Fire Engine Company and was a delegate at the Republican National Convention in Chicago in 1888. It was natural that the bank's presidents also served their communities, as county supervisors, recorders, city council members, and board of education trustees, among other community involvements.

The Bank of Stockton's rich history exemplifies the strong values and traditions that continue to guide the bank today. Headquartered on East Miner Avenue in Stockton, with 16 branch offices in contiguous market areas, the bank has a financial footprint that spans five counties. Its four Stockton branches include the Headquarters Office, the Main Street Office, the Carson Oaks Office, and the Quail Lakes Delta Office, with additional branches located in the surrounding cities of Angels Camp, Lodi, Manteca, Oakdale, Pine Grove, Ripon, Rio Vista, and Tracy. As divisions of the Bank of Stockton, Elk Grove Commerce Bank, Modesto Commerce Bank, and Turlock Commerce Bank bring the tradition of strength and service to customers in Elk Grove as well as throughout Stanislaus County.

As the Bank of Stockton approaches $2 billion in assets, it retains all the attributes of a small community bank, delivering personal service as its highest priority. Long-tenured employees are the cornerstone of the bank's strength, providing generations of customers and businesses the familiar faces they depend upon for their banking needs.

The Bank of Stockton is the oldest bank in California still operating under its original charter. This longevity was made possible by the implementation of prudent business practices and a belief in providing customers with the latest in banking conveniences brought about by technology. The Bank of Stockton, with its divisions, has been known as an industry leader in technology. From being the first bank in Stockton to provide copies of cancelled checks to its customers through their bank statements, to offering Internet banking with check images, to offering remote deposit to business customers, and now to providing mobile banking through text messaging, the Bank of Stockton is undoubtedly committed to bringing its customers the banking channels they demand.

Through the use of Internet banking and mobile banking, the Bank of Stockton is open around the clock. Its electronic deposit technology uses remote deposit capture, allowing business customers to make deposits quickly and safely from their own office by scanning checks into their personal computer and sending them to the bank electronically. This means no more trips to the bank to make deposits and no more waiting in line. The bank even installs the necessary software and offers ongoing support.

Community Involvement at Its Best

The Bank of Stockton believes that an educated public is a key component for a healthy community. Eugene Wilhoit, the bank's president in the 1920s, was a graduate of what was then the College of the Pacific in San Jose, California. In 1922 he was elected to the college's board of regents, and was instrumental in having the school moved to Stockton in 1925 (its name became University of the Pacific in 1961). R. L. Eberhardt, who became bank president in 1949,

was a longtime member of the university's board of regents, as was his son, Robert M. Eberhardt, who became president in 1963. The bank's president, Douglass M. Eberhardt, who graduated from the College of the Pacific in 1959, has been a member of the University of the Pacific Board of Regents since 2000. The Eberhardt family and the Bank of Stockton have been a driving force behind the success of the bank and the university, endowing the business school, Eberhardt School of Business, which is one of the top-ranked schools in the state.

The Bank of Stockton and its divisions are known for their tireless efforts to improve their communities through donations to numerous nonprofit organizations as well as its employee

volunteers, many of whom serve on various boards and charities. The Bank of Stockton's employees believe in working hard to make their communities better places in which to live.

Overall, the Bank of Stockton and its divisions are pillars of strength in the communities they serve. The tradition that began shortly after the Civil War, when the bank was opened—"Always with the safety of the depositors in mind"—in addition to community involvement, has continued to serve this 141-year-old institution well. Here yesterday, here today, and here tomorrow, the Bank of Stockton will continue to make history with its progressive banking technologies, always with the needs of its customers and local communities in mind.

Far left: The Bank of Stockton's location at 301 East Main Street, formerly the Stockton Savings and Loan Society, was built in 1908 and was the first skyscraper in Stockton. The building is a Stockton landmark and is listed on the National Register of Historic Places. Left: Shown here on December 21, 2006, are Eberhardt family members and Bank of Stockton employees at the ribbon-cutting ceremony for the newest branch in the Bank of Stockton family of banks—the Elk Grove Commerce Bank. From left are Trisha Brown, Margaret Eberhardt, Mimi Eberhardt, Leslie-Ann Brown, Jack E. Carter, Joan Mell Snider, MacKenzie Mell Snider, Allison Clare Eberhardt, Mary-Elizabeth Eberhardt-Sandstrom, Thomas H. Shaffer, and Douglass M. Eberhardt.

Bank of Agriculture & Commerce

This family-owned institution has been providing comprehensive financial and banking services to area businesses, professionals, and individuals since 1965. It offers a variety of deposit accounts and loan products, as well as business-related services, custom-tailored to fit each client's specific needs.

In 1965 Bank of Agriculture & Commerce (BAC) opened its first branch in downtown Brentwood, and more than 43 years later the bank has grown to become one of California's premier community banks. BAC is proud to offer a unique blend of technology services backed by employees dedicated to giving their customers an exceptional banking experience. BAC satisfies all its customers' banking needs, whether customers walk into a neighborhood branch for personal one-on-one service or bank online.

Headquartered in Stockton, BAC distinguishes itself from other banks through its approach to customer service. The bank's president and owner, CEO, and employees really know their customers. And they believe this is a very important part of their job.

The bank's expertise lies in its ability to personalize and customize its products and services to meet the needs of its customers. BAC offers state-of-the-art electronic banking products and cash management services. The bank is well positioned to service the credit and operational needs of small to large businesses, from corporations to sole proprietors. BAC also offers a wide variety of consumer banking products to satisfy the personal banking and investment needs of the business owners and their employees.

BAC has seen steady growth since it began operations in East Contra Costa County in 1965. The first Stockton branch opened in 1968, and by 2008 the branch network had grown to 10 branches in San Joaquin, Stanislaus, and East Contra Costa counties.

In 2006 the bank changed the name of the East Contra Costa branches to ECC Bank, a division of Bank of Agriculture & Commerce. The new name reflects the bank's heritage as East Contra Costa's oldest community bank. BAC branches are located in Stockton, Modesto, and Lodi, while ECC Bank branches are in Antioch, Brentwood, Concord, Discovery Bay, and Oakley. BAC customers may use any ECC branch office or ATM to conduct business and personal transactions.

The Berberian family, who owns the bank, is committed to providing the best in financial and banking services. This dedication to BAC and ECC Bank's clients is reflected throughout the daily operation of the bank.

In the tradition of community banking, it is important to everyone at BAC and ECC Bank that the customers know that the bank is financially secure and well positioned to withstand the challenges facing the banking industry. The entire bank staff is proud to report that the bank's financial performance ranks above peer banks in many important benchmarks. The bank is rated a Five Star Superior Bank by Bauer Financial and a Super Premier Bank in California by the Findley Reports.

Member FDIC • Equal Housing Lender

PROFILES OF COMPANIES AND ORGANIZATIONS
Economic Development

San Joaquin County Employment and Economic Development Department

This multifaceted department provides employment and training opportunities to job seekers in San Joaquin County and supports the business community by providing assistance with financing and many important resources and services designed to foster business start-ups, development, and expansion.

The San Joaquin County Employment and Economic Development Department (SJC EEDD) does business as the lead agency for San Joaquin County WorkNet. WorkNet is a collaboration of workforce and economic development agencies committed to fostering business and employment growth throughout the county and cities of Escalon, Lathrop, Lodi, Manteca, Ripon, Stockton, and Tracy. As existing local businesses create approximately 80 percent of all new jobs in the county, WorkNet's ongoing support and assistance to these businesses is critical for the region's economic prosperity.

Aid in Seeking Employment

WorkNet's one-stop service delivery system offers valuable information and services to job seekers and employers. WorkNet Centers, conveniently located in Stockton, Lodi, Manteca, and Tracy, provide easy access to workforce and economic development services throughout San Joaquin County.

Job seekers may attend free job-search workshops, explore career options, access the Internet for job listings, update their skills through online training, and receive assistance with résumés and cover letters from WorkNet's professional staff. The WorkNet Center provides job seekers with access to computers, telephones, and fax machines to search for employment. WorkNet also offers information about unemployment insurance; assistance in locating supportive services; information on employment for veterans; employment and training programs; and access to public housing and employment information. Young job seekers can access valuable job search tools and tips as well as information on educational opportunities and financial aid.

WorkNet supplies detailed descriptions of its partners and services on its Web site (www.sjcworknet.org).

Services for Employers

The San Joaquin County Economic Development Association (EDA) also conducts business as a WorkNet partner. Working with chambers of commerce, WorkNet serves as a one-stop business resource committed to meeting the needs of development prospects, local businesses, and the community. The EDA is a valuable resource for anyone who is starting a business, applying for a business loan, hiring additional employees, expanding a business, seeking a permit, or performing other business expansion tasks.

The EDA and WorkNet offer services, including business finance programs, to help companies remain and expand in San Joaquin County. Through the San Joaquin County Revolving Loan Fund (RLF), EDA offers business loans from $25,000 to $1 million with fixed rates and flexible terms ranging from five to 15 years. Businesses may use the funds for working capital, equipment,

SAN JOAQUIN COUNTY
ENTERPRISE ZONE

leasehold improvements, and the purchase of land or buildings. EDA also operates the Business Incubator Loan Program, which offers loans to businesses with financing needs below the RLF minimum of $25,000 through a partnership with the Small Business Development Center (SBDC).

EDA and WorkNet provide numerous programs that foster the growth and prosperity of local businesses in San Joaquin County. The EDA Business Retention and Expansion services focus on business planning, loan packaging, exporting and importing, government procurement, accounting systems, identifying local customers and suppliers,

and employee training and hiring. Through WorkNet's Employee Outreach and Recruitment Program, businesses can identify their employment needs and work with staff to recruit and screen qualified applicants. The WorkNet Assessment Center provides employee-candidate testing for interests, aptitudes, and skill levels to determine an individual's potential as an employee. WorkNet also works with employers to design and conduct job training to suit their specific needs. WorkNet's Rapid Response program provides assistance to businesses that are facing a layoff or are downsizing their workforce, changing their skill mix, or anticipating a business closure.

San Joaquin County Enterprise Zone

Designed to encourage business expansion and retention in economically distressed areas, the state granted 15-year Enterprise Zone status to San Joaquin County in January of 2008. The San Joaquin County Enterprise Zone is one of only 42 enterprise zones designated throughout California. The zone covers more than 638 square miles in the county including portions of the cities of Stockton, Lodi, Tracy, Lathrop, and Manteca. Businesses that locate or expand within the enterprise zone can substantially reduce operating costs by accessing a variety of state tax incentives and local benefits. Enterprise Zone state tax incentives include hiring credits, sales and use tax credits, business expense deductions, net operating loss (NOL) carryover, and net interest deduction for lenders. In addition to the tax incentives for businesses, the San Joaquin County

Enterprise Zone offers favorably priced improved and unimproved properties, a semiskilled and skilled workforce, and a network of public and private agencies and organizations committed to providing companies with a pro-business environment. More information about the San Joaquin County Enterprise Zone is available on its Web site at www.sjcez.org.

Business Publications

A number of publications are available from SJC WorkNet: *The Occupational Outlook Report 2006, The Comprehensive Economic Development Strategy Report 2003,* the *Community Resource Directory Brochure, The Job Developer's Association Directory of Services,* the *Five-Year Workforce Investment System Plan, SJC Workforce Investment Board Policies and Strategies,* and the *Business Primer 2000*—a comprehensive directory of business agencies in San Joaquin County.

Above left: The San Joaquin County Economic Development Association (EDA) provides services for employers such as business incentives financing; financial analysis; business training; building and site availability; labor market information; referrals to business assistance programs; regional economic development studies; and employee recruitment and training. Above right: San Joaquin County offers one of the largest enterprise zones in the state of California, providing huge incentives for business growth.

San Joaquin Partnership

This nonprofit private-public economic development organization assists businesses and industry worldwide and in the region to locate or expand in San Joaquin County, California—including the cities of Escalon, Lathrop, Lodi, Manteca, Ripon, Stockton, and Tracy—providing valuable location, marketing, and outreach strategies.

Right, both photos: One of the San Joaquin Partnership's greatest successes is the creation of a "NUMMI Cluster"—the location of 10 auto parts manufacturers that supply New United Motor Manufacturing, Inc. (NUMMI) in Fremont. Among NUMMI's suppliers is Kyoho Manufacturing of California (KHMCA), which was assisted by the San Joaquin Partnership in achieving a precedent-setting six-month schedule for the construction of its new plant in Stockton. A grand opening ceremony, shown here, was held on May 12, 2008. NUMMI produces General Motors' Pontiac Vibe sports wagon and Toyota's Corolla sedan and Tacoma truck.

The San Joaquin Partnership was formed in 1991 to help shape San Joaquin County's economic future. At that time, the region was grappling with high unemployment, increasing poverty levels, a lack of cohesiveness amongst the municipalities, and a poor or nonexistent image.

As part of a forward-looking vision for the community, a public–private partnership was formed to develop an organization that would actively market to recruit new business and industry to the county. The San Joaquin Partnership, a private nonprofit economic development corporation, has made a profound economic impact on the area.

Since its inception, the San Joaquin Partnership has successfully provided services to more than 307 companies that chose to locate or expand in San Joaquin County. These company locations have resulted in the cumulative creation of more than 49,000 new jobs providing an annual labor income of $2.2 billion.

Michael Locke, president and CEO of the San Joaquin Partnership, says that the organization has experienced a high level of success unmatched by other California economic development corporations.

"We have an aggressive marketing and outreach program that makes us more proactive than reactive," says Locke. "We spend the time necessary to meet with company executives, real estate brokers, and site consultants to familiarize them on a personal level with what San Joaquin County has to offer in terms of its transportation network, available industrial and commercial space, incentives such as the Enterprise Zone, and workforce capabilities. Our materials are top-notch; current and informative without a lot of fluff."

He says the San Joaquin Partnership provides the county and its seven cities with marketing and outreach strategies and the region is presented as a unified entity, something the

San Joaquin Partnership has worked hard to promote.

Locke says that the San Joaquin Partnership's focus is to attract new companies, while assisting local industry with expansions or new location needs. He points out that the staff works on about 100 active projects at any given time and strives to site at least 15 to 20 of these annually.

"In 2007, we were successful with 15 business projects, and of these, five were retention projects—companies that chose to stay and expand in the community rather than leave for another region of California or even a different state," says Locke.

He says one of the largest new location projects is USG Corporation's decision to locate a new $260 million manufacturing facility at the Port of Stockton. The San Joaquin Partnership had worked on this project for more than two years and provided the company with all the assistance necessary, including coordinating incentives, that USG needed to make an informed decision.

According to USG officials, they could not have embarked on such a venture without the assistance and the vision of the San Joaquin Partnership. "They have been invaluable in helping us work through a host of issues, including site selection, environmental compliance, labor force recruitment, logistics and transportation analysis, and an incentive package that made this project possible," explains Dan Salisbury, USG vice president of real estate. He continues to say that the San Joaquin Partnership recognizes that everyone in the Central Valley benefits when government

and business work together to build a healthy, growing economy.

Locke explains that the San Joaquin Partnership is able to fully demonstrate the benefits of a San Joaquin County location—that it is a key entry point to the global gateway network connecting through the Bay Area to the Pacific Rim and beyond. Additionally, it is central to the marketplace of the West Coast and of California—the world's eighth-largest economy by gross domestic product, according to the World Bank.

Locke adds, "We emphasize that you can do business in California—if you come to San Joaquin County!" He says the San Joaquin Partnership, which

maintains a high level of confidentiality with its clients, can provide a company with all the data, but the client's ultimate location choice is based on market, workforce, competitive position, and land or building opportunities.

Locke is proud that after nearly two decades of striving to bring San Joaquin County to the forefront in the hunt for better jobs and wages for its residents, the San Joaquin Partnership and the county have developed a positive image where once there was none. Now when he walks into a decision maker's office or meets with site consultants at a conference, he says, "They know who we are."

Above left: Michael E. Locke is president and CEO of the San Joaquin Partnership. Above right: This rendering shows the new $260 million, environmentally responsible manufacturing plant being built by USG Corporation at the Port of Stockton, scheduled for completion in 2012.

Greater Stockton Chamber of Commerce

For more than a century, this highly proactive organization has promoted the economic vitality of the greater Stockton community. It provides strong business-development programs and advocacy—including regulatory, permitting, and workforce matters—for its member businesses, small and large.

The Greater Stockton Chamber of Commerce was founded in 1901 when the city of Stockton was largely an agricultural hub of about 18,000 people. It has been an integral part of the city's explosive transformation into a thriving community of 289,927 people, in a county of nearly 685,660 residents.

While agriculture remains a vital part of Stockton and the Central Valley's economy, the Greater Stockton Chamber has played an essential role in helping to diversify the economy of Stockton and San Joaquin County.

Mission

The mission of the Greater Stockton Chamber is to aggressively develop and promote an economically vibrant business community. It has developed several programs designed to help its members succeed. Some programs serve as business advocates and watchdogs; they are designed to improve the local business environment for the future of all members. Other programs are designed to directly help members with their day-to-day operations and marketing efforts.

Advocacy Programs

The Greater Stockton Chamber works on behalf of its membership through a variety of advocacy efforts.

The Government Relations Council (GRC) works on behalf of members to increase the Greater Stockton Chamber's influence with various legislative agencies and their staff members in ways that are specific and measurable. Its projects include identifying key issues, gathering membership input, and developing policy statements; communicating and advocating positions to appropriate parties; and publishing elected officials' voting records correlated with the chamber's policy statements.

The Small Business Council (SBC) and the Manufacturers Industrial Distribution Roundtable (MIDR) act as advocates for members within the chamber and the community, delivering educational programs targeted to their business needs. The SBC acts on behalf of small-to-midsize businesses, and the MIDR provides information and advocacy for larger businesses.

Member Programs

Numerous programs of the Greater Stockton Chamber directly serve members' ongoing activities.

Green Team San Joaquin is one of the largest of these programs. It is a public/private partnership designed to enhance the delivery of Greater Stockton Chamber services and to address economical and environmental development issues within San Joaquin County. The purposes of

Green Team San Joaquin are to streamline recycling and economic efforts, enhance communication between the public and private sectors pertaining to business attraction and retention in San Joaquin County, and promote programs to show the general public environmentally sound technologies for reducing, reusing, and recycling, to achieve better environmental and economic efficiencies.

The Stockton Chamber Apprenticeship Program (SCAP) is designed to assist efforts to place unemployed CalWORKs clients into the San Joaquin County workforce. SCAP helps to reduce the number of San Joaquin County residents receiving public assistance.

The Business Education Alliance (BEA) provides the means by which employers and educators work together to understand each other's needs and requirements. The goal of the BEA is to improve students' educational outcomes and prepare students for the workplace.

Leadership Stockton—California's oldest adult community leadership program—was created to inspire a new generation of men and women ready to assume leadership roles in the community. It challenges and prepares individuals from diverse backgrounds to become influential in the region's future.

Events

The Greater Stockton Chamber hosts a variety of events each year to help members become more involved with the community and to spread the word about their businesses and services.

The Annual ATHENA Award event recognizes an outstanding businesswoman who can serve as a role model for all women. Winners are honored for their professional accomplishments, community service, and role in helping other women in the community attain success.

The Industrial and Technology Barbecue is an annual event at which the Greater Stockton Chamber toasts new or expanded manufacturers, technological companies, and industries located in San Joaquin County.

The State of the City, cosponsored by the City of Stockton, is a high-profile event held during the mayor's annual address. It showcases the city's economic, educational, and cultural development, as well as plans for upcoming projects. Concurrent with the event is a trade show, providing an ideal opportunity for members to learn of the many local and state programs available to assist all businesses, as well as to appreciate the value of Stockton's strategic location for serving not only local customers but also a national and international clientele.

Stockton Conference & Visitors Bureau (CVB), a division of the Greater Stockton Chamber, is the destination-marketing organization for Stockton. The CVB is funded primarily by the Tourism Business Improvement District, which provides an assessment of local hotels' revenues from overnight guest stays. The CVB focuses on increasing hotels' overnight stays by marketing to leisure travelers, meeting and conference planners, and group tour companies. It also has an important mission of keeping residents up-to-date on the many and diverse opportunities available in Stockton and the surrounding area for enjoying their community full-time.

This page: The Stockton Conference & Visitors Bureau, a division of the Greater Stockton Chamber, publicizes the extensive travel and leisure events and activities in Stockton and the surrounding area—including (at left, and clockwise) the Stockton Symphony, paddleboating at the Stockton Asparagus Festival, fine art and fine dining at the Downtown Art Walk, a performance at the Bob Hope Theatre, and an afternoon at the ballpark.

Downtown Stockton Alliance

Committed to the redevelopment of Downtown Stockton, this nonprofit organization is successfully attracting new and expanding companies to the area and effectively maintaining a vibrant entertainment district that appeals to tourists, residents, and downtown workers.

Over the last 10 years, the landscape of Downtown Stockton has changed dramatically. New buildings have been raised on empty lots, and historic structures have been renovated. Crime has decreased by more than 50 percent, and millions of public and private dollars have been invested in parks and plazas, sports venues, an entertainment district, retail and dining establishments, and housing and hotel properties. The waterfront is alive with real estate projects such as the Sheraton Stockton Hotel at Regent Pointe, Paragary's Bar and Grill at the Hotel Stockton, and the Morelli Park Boat Launching Facility.

The catalyst for this activity is the Downtown Stockton Alliance, a public and private partnership of 250 property owners and 1,300 downtown businesses

that has spurred the development of the area into an urban hot spot featuring historic architecture, cultural attractions, and a thriving business community. Created in 1996, the alliance is clearly accomplishing its mission: "To develop, promote, and maintain historic Downtown Stockton as a regional business, cultural, and entertainment destination."

The responsibilities of the alliance are diverse. The organization serves as the collective voice for downtown businesses and property owners through public policy and advocacy; brings new business and helps to retain existing business within the area; coordinates marketing, promotions, and special events to increase the appeal of Downtown Stockton; publishes *The Downtowner* newspaper, with timely

information on events, real estate, and more; provides Hospitality Guides, who focus on safety, customer service, and business success by offering visitors directions, information, and historic tours assistance; and provides maintenance for the 90-block area, including daily litter removal and the steam cleaning and pressure washing of sidewalks.

In true downtown fashion, the heart of Stockton is full of things to see and do. Stockton Ballpark at Banner Island and the Stockton Arena host baseball, hockey, arena football, and professional soccer. The Bob Hope Theatre offers concerts and classic films, and the Janet Leigh Plaza features movies, free concerts, and street performers. Additional highlights include the Children's Museum of Stockton, the Weber Point Events

Center; the Dean DeCarli Waterfront Square; an Art Walk on the second Friday of every month; and the Farmers Market on Fridays, from 9 a.m. to 2 p.m.

Now the City of Stockton and the alliance are working on a jointly initiated project to comprehensively rebrand Downtown Stockton. The project is designed to increase local civic pride and to fully activate the downtown through evening activities and celebrations. Stockton will be working to earn the reputation as the place to celebrate in the Central Valley by recruiting local and major events to be held downtown.

Overall, the work of the Downtown Stockton Alliance has led to unprecedented growth—today businesses in Downtown Stockton provide employment for 20,000 workers. Designated as both an enterprise zone and a redevelopment zone, the area offers many business incentives as well as the benefit of hundreds of annual events that bring the community together and strengthen the economy. Through its efforts in reinventing Downtown Stockton, the alliance brings considerable energy and prosperity to the city.

PROFILES OF COMPANIES AND ORGANIZATIONS
Education

University of the Pacific

This university, the first to be chartered in California, has a long tradition of educational innovation and excellence, in which academic rigor, dedicated faculty members, small class sizes, practical experience, community engagement, and a vibrant residential life combine to create superior learning.

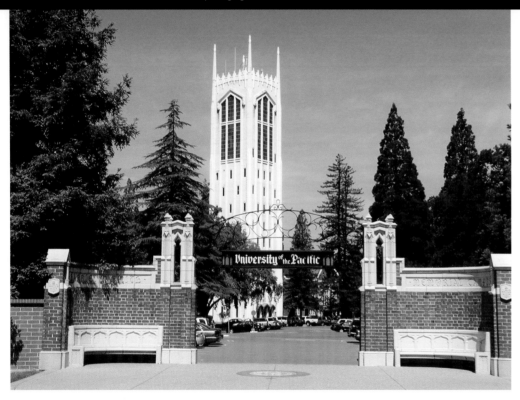

Above: The Robert E. Burns Tower, once the tallest building in Stockton, houses the University of the Pacific's welcome center and the carillon.

The University of the Pacific is located in north Stockton on a luxuriantly landscaped campus graced with Gothic architecture. Combining the intimacy of a small college with the resources of a comprehensive university, Pacific— as the university is popularly known— attracts top faculty and high-achieving students from across the country and around the world. The oldest chartered university in California, Pacific was founded in Santa Clara in 1851 and was moved to Stockton in 1923.

Pacific remains the only major private university in the Central Valley.

Pacific has more than 6,000 students on its three campuses. The Stockton campus includes about 4,600 students in its College of the Pacific, the Conservatory of Music, the Gladys L. Benerd School of Education, the Eberhardt School of Business, the School of Engineering and Computer Science, the School of International Studies, and the Thomas J. Long School of Pharmacy and Health Sciences. On the Sacramento campus, the Pacific McGeorge School of Law enrolls about 1,100 students. On the San Francisco campus is the Arthur A. Dugoni School of Dentistry, which enrolls approximately 500 students.

Educational Value

Pacific is known for top-tier professional schools in dentistry, law, and pharmacy. The Conservatory of Music, the oldest music conservatory in the West, graduated Dave Brubeck and hundreds of other professional musicians and composers. Pacific also offers strong programs in biology, chemistry, international studies, business, engineering, and other fields.

Pacific has been listed as one of the top 50 "Best Values" by *U.S.News & World Report* since 2001 and is consistently ranked among the top 100 national doctoral universities. Its 55,000 living alumni include internationally renowned composer and jazz pianist Brubeck (class of 1942) and his wife, librettist Iola Whitlock Brubeck (class of 1945); astronaut José Hernández (class of 1984); and numerous prominent business leaders, educators, judges, artists, athletes, writers, diplomats, and government leaders.

A Stockton Landmark

Pacific's 175-acre Stockton campus is modeled after East Coast universities. Students learn in an inspirational setting of ivy-covered red brick buildings set in open quadrangles amid lush greenery. Originally landscaped by John McLaren, designer of San Francisco's Golden Gate Park, the campus grounds contain more than 100 varieties of trees and plants.

Photo, this page: © Gail Matsui
Photos, opposite page: Left, © Larry Maglott; center, © Kent Lacin; right, © Steve Puppe

The Robert E. Burns Tower, once the tallest building in Stockton, fills the courtyards with music from its carillon twice a day. Morris Chapel, with rich stained-glass windows, is one of the most beautiful chapels in the area and a popular venue for weddings.

The campus also has provided the setting for a number of Hollywood films, including *Raiders of the Lost Ark.*

A Community Resource

For the campus and larger community, Pacific brings prominent world leaders and scholars to speak on campus; presents concerts, operas, plays, and art exhibits; and screens popular, classic, special interest, and foreign films throughout the year. The Brubeck Institute's annual Brubeck Festival features academic symposia and concerts by renowned jazz musicians, vocalists, students, and faculty members.

University health care clinics offer services for residents, and there are also health fairs and information symposia on important health issues. Students and faculty and staff members contribute thousands of volunteer hours annually to area charities. The Center for Professional and Continuing Education offers degree and certificate programs, continuing education, and personal enrichment courses for lifelong learning. Pacific centers and institutes dedicated to an array of topics work toward solutions to local and regional issues

through community partnerships, education, and research.

Pacific's libraries contain more than 700,000 books and periodicals. The Holt-Atherton Special Collections department houses manuscript collections, a specialized book collection, and the university archives, including the manuscripts and published essays of naturalist John Muir and the complete archive of Dave and Iola Brubeck. Nonstudent community members may purchase a library card.

The Pacific Experience

Pacific offers strong academic programs in more than 80 programs of study leading to bachelor's, master's, and doctoral degrees and to educational credentials. Accelerated programs facilitate earning undergraduate and graduate degrees in fewer years than comparable programs in business, education, law, and the health sciences. A comprehensive financial aid program makes Pacific's quality education accessible to students of all economic backgrounds.

Small classes and a focus on teaching promote close faculty-student interaction. The Pacific experience combines

academic excellence with real-world learning—internships, study abroad, undergraduate research, and community service—which is designed to prepare individuals for lasting achievements and responsible leadership in their careers and communities.

The university provides full information about all its programs and activities on its Web site (www.pacific.edu).

Nearly 60 percent of Pacific students live on campus and participate in a vibrant residential life, which offers more than 125 student clubs and organizations and a comprehensive recreational program. The Pacific Tigers compete in NCAA Division I sports as a member of the Big West Conference, with seven men's teams and nine women's teams. The Pacific Tigers have accumulated 23 conference athletic championships and 52 NCAA tournament appearances, and more than 1,100 students have been named Big West Scholar-Athletes.

Left: Pacific's collegiate Gothic architecture and well-landscaped grounds bring the beauty of the eastern Ivy League to California's Central Valley. Above left: The largest majors at Pacific are in the sciences, supporting strong pre–health science and engineering programs and offering a wide range of opportunities in undergraduate research. Above right: Local fans support the Pacific Tigers' 16 NCAA Division I athletics teams, which compete in the Big West Conference.

St. Mary's High School combines academic excellence and comprehensive high school courses and activities with the values-based tradition of Catholic teachings and service. The four-year, coeducational school helps students achieve self-discipline along with personal, spiritual, and academic growth.

Catholic education is part of the fabric of Stockton. When the generous and determined founder of the City of Stockton, Captain Charles M. Weber, and his wife, Helen, connected with the visionary priest William Bernard O'Connor, the outcome was Catholic education in the young, bustling port city. One of Stockton's first Catholic high schools, St. Agnes Academy, was dedicated in 1876 by another historic figure, Archbishop Joseph S. Alemany.

A new girls' school was built in 1914, St. Agnes High School. In 1918, boys were admitted to the high school program. In 1927, the boys got their own school, the new St. Mary's High School. With the Great Depression beginning in 1929, the community could not support two Catholic high schools, so the two schools were consolidated in 1930 at St. Mary's.

By the 1950s, St. Mary's was ready to expand. It moved to a 25-acre campus in north Stockton, opening in 1956 with an enrollment of 518 students. The new school had four classroom wings, a library, cafeteria, chapel, and three athletic fields. By 1961, the school had added a gymnasium/auditorium, a student chapel, a friary, and a convent. The new campus saw many successes through the years, graduating thousands of students who went on to become the parents, educators, business people, professionals, and workers of the San Joaquin Valley.

With the school's 50th anniversary at the current location approaching, its leaders announced a major building and renovation plan. The Lagorio Family Library/Technology and Administration Building—with 23,000 square feet for the library, counseling services, administrative and business offices, faculty areas, and classrooms—became operational for the 2006–2007 school year. The Cortopassi Aquatics Center was dedicated in October 2007. Additional construction and renovation are in progress.

Today, 1,159 students learn and grow at St. Mary's, guided by a faculty and staff of 94, including five who belong to religious communities. The student body is diverse, with 48 percent from African American, Hispanic, Asian, and Native American backgrounds. Students take courses in religion, English, social studies, mathematics, physical education and health, science, computers, foreign language, fine arts, and other electives. Students can take college courses at Delta Community College and the University of the Pacific, both of which are relatively nearby.

Academic excellence is evidenced in a variety of ways. College-level Advanced Placement (AP) courses are offered in nine subjects. Students excel in the AP program, with St. Mary's exceeding state and national averages since 1990. The Class of 2007 had 27 National AP Scholars.

St. Mary's is fully accredited by the Western Association of Schools and Colleges and by the Western Catholic Education Association. Graduates of the Class of 2007 were accepted at more than 42 colleges and universities and earned awards and scholarships totaling more than $5.9 million.

Athletics is a major part of student life. St. Mary's Rams compete in many sports, including football, men's and women's badminton, baseball, men's and women's basketball, men's and women's cross-country, men's and women's golf, men's and women's soccer, softball, men's and women's swimming, men's and women's tennis, men's and women's track and field, women's volleyball, men's and women's water polo, and wrestling. The Rams are Tri-City Athletic League (TCAL) champions in football, women's volleyball, men's water polo, and women's tennis. An exuberant student cheering section, wearing green and white, boosts school spirit at games.

Performing arts groups and other clubs provide countless hours of learning and service opportunities as well as enjoyment. The student newspaper, the *Kettle,* reports the activities and issues on campus and beyond. The yearbook, the *Cauldron,* tracks the highlights of each school year. Major plays are staged each semester, including the Tony Award–winning *Into the Woods* for spring 2008 and *The Man Who Came to Dinner* for fall 2007. Music students have choir and band options.

Whatever a student's interests, St. Mary's 28 clubs and organizations have something to offer. Many involve service, such as the Christian Relief Outreach Project (CROP) and Campus Ministry, or educational enrichment, such as Science Club and the Ram Computer Club.

Today, as it was in 1876, Catholic education in Stockton is a dream come true for Catholic families. St. Mary's High School is a mainstay in the Catholic education system.

Above left: The St. Mary's High School student chapel provides a place for students to gather, worship, and reflect.
Above right: This artist's rendering depicts St. Mary's proposed science center.

For more than 70 years San Joaquin Delta College has been providing the Central Valley with a better-educated workforce, as well as benefiting local businesses and stimulating the economy. For students seeking advancement to a four-year college, vocational training that leads to a new career, or noncredit classes to expand their horizons, Delta College promises an excellent and affordable education.

Located in Stockton, California, Delta College accommodates the needs of several surrounding communities, including Lodi, Manteca, Tracy, and Galt, as well as numerous foothill towns. Classes are taught not only at the Stockton campus but also in designated public schools and other easily accessible locations throughout the region.

The school offers associate in arts and associate in science degrees and a full range of more than 100 career and technical education certificate programs in fields relevant to today's economy. Through collaborative agreements with major companies, such as Caterpillar and General Motors, specialized training is provided as well as employment opportunities.

Among Delta College's many educational opportunities designed to prepare students for immediate employment are programs in police work, firefighting, nursing, and emergency medical services, through which thousands of students have gained professional training.

Centers of Education

The Delta College main campus, one of the largest in California, is composed of five educational centers named after local residents who made significant contributions to education throughout their lives.

Cunningham Center, named after Thomas Cunningham, sheriff of San Joaquin County in the late 1800s, was the first center to be opened when the campus was built in the 1970s. At the Cunningham Center, classes are offered in physical and life sciences, public safety and services, and computer science. Cunningham Center is also home to the George H. Clever Planetarium.

Holt Center is named after Benjamin Holt, who helped to make possible the large-scale farming of the San Joaquin Delta's soft peat soil when he developed the belt-tread tractor, and whose Holt Manufacturing Company was one of the forerunners of Caterpillar. Opened in 1974, Holt Center is home to instruction in music, machine technology, heating and air-conditioning, welding, and engineering.

A leader in community college science education, Delta College trains future researchers by offering a certificate in

Electron Microscopy at its Center for Microscopy and Allied Sciences.

Shima Center honors George Shima, who left Japan for the United States in the 1880s and founded an agricultural empire on land he reclaimed from the San Joaquin Delta. Classes at the Shima Center, which was opened in 1975, offer instruction in agriculture and natural resources, broadcasting, fine arts, home economics, early childhood education, business, and photography. In the center is the L. H. Horton Gallery, where photography, painting, and other fine arts are displayed.

Budd Center, completed in 1976, is named after James Budd, who, as a state representative in the early 1880s, helped gather funds to dredge

the Stockton Channel. He went on to serve as governor of California from 1895 to 1899. The center houses the school's physical education facilities, including a 3,000-seat gymnasium and a 50-meter pool.

Locke Center is named after Dean Jewett Locke, a physician who came to California to find gold and ended up founding the city of Lockeford and the Lockeford School District. At the center, instruction is offered in nursing and business, as well as drama, which is supported by a 400-seat main theater and a 100-seat studio theater. The center is also home to the 1,400-seat Warren Atherton Auditorium, which features dramatic plays, musical theater, and performances by the Stockton Symphony.

A Rich Past and a Promising Future

San Joaquin Delta College is the successor to Stockton Junior College, which was formed in 1935 and became Stockton College in 1948. The college expanded its curriculum to include vocational programs in response to the Central Valley's booming population in the 1950s.

Delta College legally separated from the Stockton Unified School District (SUSD) in 1963, making the college a tenant on land owned by SUSD. At this time the college served all of San Joaquin County and parts of three other counties. In 1966 the college attempted to create its own multicampus system through a bond election, which did not pass. Another campaign succeeded in 1968, however, leading to the construction of a $50 million campus.

Today a $250 million bond measure, passed in 2004, is financing the construction of a satellite campus northwest of Tracy at Mountain House. This campus will focus on technology, engineering, and the arts. Additional projects include a planned center in Lodi as well as expansion and renewal at the Manteca Center.

The bond will also allow for Stockton campus enhancements, such as new classrooms, computer laboratories, and science laboratories, that will help accommodate the educational needs of the Central Valley's growing population. The school's new facilities combined with its comprehensive instructional programs continue the fulfillment of San Joaquin Delta College's mission and support the college's vision of the future.

Above left: Delta College's main campus, one of the largest in California, is composed of five educational centers. The design of each center includes a central courtyard and a study lounge to encourage students of different backgrounds to interact based on their common interests. Above right: An instructor guides a student in a state-of-the-art classroom at Delta College's Center for Microscopy and Allied Sciences. Delta College offers a certificate in Electron Microscopy.

California State University, Stanislaus–Stockton Center

This comprehensive public university emphasizes quality and excellence in education and supports diversity. It offers baccalaureate degrees in the liberal arts, sciences, business, and education; teaching credentials; master's degrees; and other professional studies—all designed to help students reach their full potential.

Above, all photos: California State University, Stanislaus–Stockton Center is an exceptional public university that, with its smaller size and commitment to excellence, offers benefits common to those of a private education. Acacia Court houses library access, a bookstore, game and fitness rooms, a student lounge and health services, classrooms, a computer laboratory for conducting research, and more. Historic Magnolia Mansion serves the community with art exhibits, performances, seminars, and other events.

Named one of the best 366 U.S. colleges by the Princeton Review, and one of the best colleges for educational excellence by *U.S.News & World Report*, California State University, Stanislaus (CSU Stanislaus) offers qualities and opportunities that extend to its Stockton Center—an inviting small-town atmosphere, a distinguished faculty and professional staff, and a wide variety of academic programs designed to appeal to a highly diverse student population. The main campus of CSU Stanislaus is located in Stanislaus County in Turlock, California. The university also has a campus in San Joaquin County, the CSU Stanislaus–Stockton Center, which is located near downtown Stockton in University Park.

CSU Stanislaus offers 42 undergraduate bachelor's degree programs, 24 master's degree programs, seven credential programs, five graduate certificate programs, and a Doctor of Education in Educational Leadership. Many students are attracted by preprofessional programs in law, medicine, dentistry, pharmacy, physical therapy, veterinary medicine, optometry, laboratory technology, and medical laboratory technology.

CSU Stanislaus is composed of six colleges: the College of the Arts, the College of Business Administration, the College of Education, the College of Human and Health Sciences, the College of Humanities and Social Sciences, and the College of Natural Sciences. Additional courses are available through University Extended Education courses, televised courses, and Web courses via the Internet.

Part of the CSU Stanislaus strategy is to provide students with a stimulating and rewarding environment that fosters their success. Its stated mission is "to engage every member of our campus in expanding their intellectual, creative, and social horizons in a diverse community committed to nourishing a thirst for lifelong learning." The small school atmosphere, a student-to-faculty ratio of 19 to one, and a commitment to excellence provide the benefits that are typically found in private educational institutions.

Established in 1974, the CSU Stanislaus–Stockton Center is set on a developing 102-acre site in Stockton's historic Magnolia District. CSU Stanislaus–Stockton, which is home to 10 resident faculty members, offers upper division and graduate courses that earn full academic credit toward baccalaureate and master's degrees and professional credentials. Through classes offered in Acacia Hall at the CSU Stanislaus–Stockton Center and broadcast to the site via live two-way television, most students can complete their degrees without the need to commute to the main campus in Turlock. The Stockton campus includes computer laboratories, a library access center, a student lounge, a fitness center, academic advisory services, health services, and landscaped courtyards for student and faculty gatherings.

University Park is a Grupe Company master-planned site anchored by the CSU Stanislaus–Stockton Center and designed to make the area economically vibrant. Additional options for the beautifully landscaped University Park include a government center, neighborhood school, housing, offices, and retail businesses.

Mary Stuart Rogers Educational Services Gateway Building at California State University, Stanislaus–Stockton Center

PROFILES OF COMPANIES AND ORGANIZATIONS
Energy and Utilities

Pacific Gas and Electric Company

This award-winning utility, a leader in energy conservation, supplies electricity and natural gas to 40 percent of Californians and one in 20 Americans. Using renewable energy and creating innovative environmental initiatives, it delivers some of the nation's cleanest electric power.

One of the nation's leading renewable energy providers, Pacific Gas and Electric Company (PG&E) serves northern and central California. Above left: Gas service representative Brian Roche replaces a 1950s tin gas meter with a new model. Above right: Charlie Boyle, gas crew foreman, is shown with one of PG&E's natural gas–fueled, heavy duty gas crew trucks.

Pacific Gas and Electric Company (PG&E), a subsidiary of PG&E Corporation, is one of the country's largest utilities that supply both electricity and natural gas. Its transmission and delivery network—which includes more than 140,000 miles of electricity lines and more than 45,000 miles of natural gas pipelines—meets the energy needs of about 15 million people across a 70,000-square-mile service area. In addition to delivering gas and electricity, PG&E is a nationally recognized leader in energy efficiency.

A Clean and Efficient Network

Supplying some of the country's cleanest energy to 5 percent of Americans, PG&E emits less than 1 percent of the nation's electricity-related carbon dioxide. In a typical year, more than half of the electricity PG&E delivers comes from sources that do not emit carbon dioxide. Additionally, the company is dedicated to increasing its use of renewable sources of electricity, such as wind, hydroelectric, geothermal, biomass, and solar power.

PG&E serves 5.1 million customers with electricity that it generates from plants powered by hydroelectric power, gas-fired steam, and nuclear energy. It also buys electricity from independent producers in California as well as other states. PG&E distributes natural gas it transports from California, the southwestern United States, and Canada to approximately 4.2 million customers.

PG&E operates the United States' largest investor-owned hydroelectric system, which consists of more than 100 reservoirs and 68 power-houses, generating enough clean and cost-effective power to supply electricity to nearly four million homes. Most of PG&E's reservoirs also provide public campgrounds and picnic areas.

PG&E's Diablo Canyon Power Plant supplies low-cost, emission-free electricity for more than 1.6 million homes. Since operations began in 1985, it has established a record as one of the safest and most efficient nuclear power plants in the nation, receiving high safety and performance ratings from the United States Nuclear Regulatory Commission and the Institute of Nuclear Power Operations. To maintain the safety and security of the facility, PG&E employs a highly trained, well-armed security force in addition to a seismic department, and plans to invest $1 billion in the plant by the end of the decade.

A Leader in Clean Energy

PG&E recognizes that its actions have a direct impact on the environment. As such, PG&E is a leader in energy efficiency and renewable power initiatives to reduce greenhouse gas emissions.

In 2008 the U.S. Green Building Council awarded PG&E's headquarters in San Francisco gold-level Leadership in Energy and Environmental Design (LEED) certification. Measures taken to reduce energy consumption at PG&E's other facilities include using recyclable food containers, installing energy-efficient lighting and appliances, and using advanced technology that reduces the number of computer servers needed.

PG&E owns one of the largest utility-owned fleets of natural gas vehicles. Through its Clean Air Transportation Program and its 37 natural gas fueling stations, it also encourages its customers to use natural gas vehicles. The petroleum saved by PG&E's fleet and its customers' fleets equaled more than 16.6 million gallons in 2007.

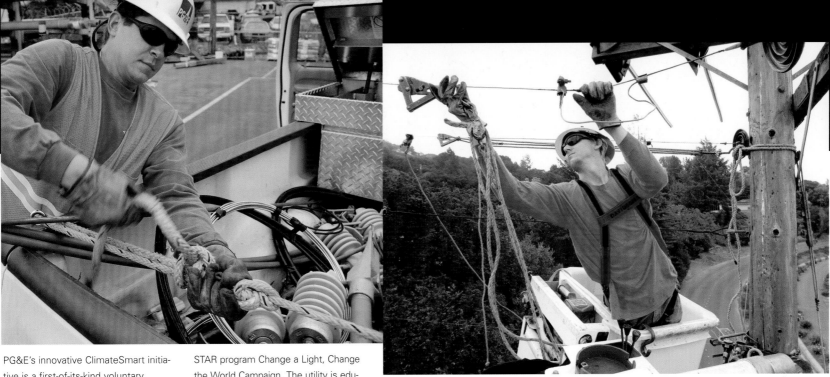

PG&E's innovative ClimateSmart initiative is a first-of-its-kind voluntary climate protection program. It gives customers an opportunity to pay a small monthly fee to fund projects that reduce greenhouse gas emissions. PG&E enrolled as the first participant in the ClimateSmart program by committing $1.5 million of shareholder funds to make all of the energy use in the company's offices, service centers, maintenance facilities, and other company buildings climate neutral.

In 2007 PG&E began a campaign to distribute one million compact fluorescent lightbulbs (CFLs) as part of the U.S. Environmental Protection Agency and U.S. Department of Energy's ENERGY STAR program Change a Light, Change the World Campaign. The utility is educating its customers about the energy efficiency of CFLs and is working with manufacturers and retailers to make these bulbs available at a discount.

PG&E's demand-response programs reward customers who voluntarily reduce their energy use during peak-demand events, and its energy audits, direct-installation programs, rebates, and incentive programs encourage its customers to use emerging energy-efficient technologies. Its Energy Training Center in Stockton educates customers about these emerging options. As a sponsor of the University of California, Davis's Energy Efficiency Center, PG&E contributes to the development of these technologies.

Recognizing the large energy needs of computer data centers, PG&E offers its high-technology customers incentives for using energy-efficient computer servers, upgrading heating and cooling systems, and using low-energy LCD monitors. In 2007 PG&E was the first utility to join the nonprofit global Green Grid consortium, which is dedicated to "advancing energy efficiency in data centers and business computing ecosystems." In 2008 PG&E formed a nationwide coalition of utilities committed to these same goals.

PG&E also works outside of California to improve energy conservation through the Edison Electric Institute's Energy Efficiency Task Force and the China–U.S. Energy Efficiency Alliance.

PG&E received an ENERGY STAR Award for Excellence and was named a Partner of the Year at the ENERGY STAR 2008 awards ceremony for its work in reducing greenhouse gas emissions through energy efficiency. As a recognized leader in energy conservation, Pacific Gas and Electric Company remains committed to supplying clean, efficient energy to its customers.

Above left: Transmission and distribution (T&D) assistant Aaron Swanson ties down a load of equipment at one of PG&E's service center yards.
Above right: PG&E lineman Tyler Davidson prepares to disconnect nonenergized and grounded lines for replacement of a damaged eight-foot wooden cross-arm, shown in the upper right corner.

Stockton Area Water Suppliers (SAWS)

This organization secures, treats, and delivers drinking water for the benefit of the residents and businesses of the Stockton Metropolitan Area. The mission of SAWS is to develop and implement strategies to help sustain the area's vigorous community with a consistently reliable supply of drinking water.

STOCKTON AREA WATER SUPPLIERS

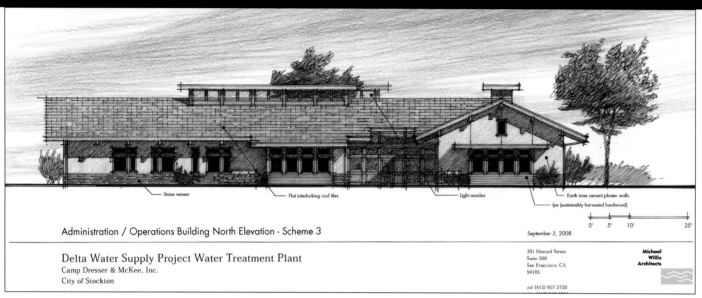

— Stone veneer
— Flat interlocking roof tiles
— Light monitor
— Earth tone cement plaster walls
— Ipe (sustainably harvested hardwood)

0'   5'   10'   25'

Administration / Operations Building North Elevation - Scheme 3

September 3, 2008

Delta Water Supply Project Water Treatment Plant
Camp Dresser & McKee, Inc.
City of Stockton

301 Howard Street
Suite 500
San Francisco, CA
94105

Michael Willis Architects

tel: (415) 957 2750

Above: The Delta Water Supply Project water treatment plant will create a new water source for the City of Stockton by routing water from the Sacramento–San Joaquin Delta.

The Sacramento–San Joaquin Delta is central to California's water distribution system—two-thirds of all of the state's residents and millions of acres of irrigated farmland rely on the Delta for clean water. Serving the San Francisco Bay Area, the Silicon Valley, the San Joaquin Valley, the Central Coast, and southern California, the Delta supplies drinking water for 25 million people, supporting urban and rural uses, including the state's $27 billion agricultural industry.

Over time, competing demands for water have challenged the Delta's ability to continue its starring role. The estuary—the West Coast's largest—is in need of long-term solutions to ensure reliable, quality water supplies and a healthy ecosystem.

Responding to this urgent need is the Stockton Area Water Suppliers (SAWS), an organization composed of a water wholesaler—Stockton East Water District (SEWD)—and three water retailers: the

City of Stockton, San Joaquin County, and California Water Service Company. The mission of SAWS is to ensure the sustainability and long-term reliability of drinking water for the Stockton Metropolitan Area through supportive communication and assistance of their individual and joint water projects.

Three projects have been implemented by SAWS members to assure Stockton's long-term water reliability. The Delta Water Supply Project

(DWSP) focuses on a dependable way to bring additional water to the City; the MORE WATER Project and the Farmington Groundwater Recharge & Seasonal Habitat Program address the needs of the common overdrafted groundwater basin used by both a $2 billion agricultural industry and the Stockton Metropolitan Area.

The Delta Water Supply Project

The Sacramento–San Joaquin Delta covers more than 738,000 acres in five counties. The Sacramento and San Joaquin rivers come together in the Delta before they flow to San Francisco Bay and out to the ocean. The Delta is home to more than 750 plant and animal species, and its unique ecosystem supports 20 endangered species.

DWSP will create a new supplemental source of water for the Stockton Metropolitan Area by routing water from the Delta through miles of pipeline installed along Eight Mile Road. Once there, the water will be pumped to a state-of-the-art surface water treatment plant where it will be treated according to the highest drinking water standards and then distributed.

The water treatment plant will be located just north of Eight Mile Road on Lower Sacramento Road and will be designed in such a way as to complement nearby surroundings. The plant site will include an administration/operations building, a membrane building, a maintenance shop, and other treatment process–related facilities.

The site will be oriented in such a way as to maximize the future potential use of the remainder of the 126-acre City-owned parcel. In consideration of current and future neighbors, a generous landscape buffer will be included around the perimeter of the site.

In keeping with the City of Stockton's green building policy, the administration/operations building will strive for Leadership in Energy and Environmental Design (LEED) Silver Certification, and all other buildings will incorporate appropriate sustainable materials and design concepts.

The MORE WATER Project

Today there are approximately 650,000 residents in San Joaquin County (SJC), and the population is expected to double by 2040. A concern raised by this projection is the fact that much of the region's water flows outside the area for use in other counties. The MORE WATER Project, developed under a partnership between SJC and the U.S. Bureau of Reclamation, is needed to assure sustainable water supplies for current and future residents and to provide additional surface water capacity.

The strategies that are outlined by the MORE WATER Project are projected to provide the following benefits: up to 125,000 acre-feet per year of new water supply from the Mokelumne River; up to 10 megawatts per year of new hydropower supply; a decrease in groundwater overdraft (shortage); reduced saline intrusion into the basin; and an increase in water supply reliability for SJC.

The Farmington Groundwater Recharge & Seasonal Habitat Program

Every year agricultural and urban water use exceeds the natural recharge capacity in the SEWD service area by as much as 135,000 acre-feet. This leads to the closure of urban wells due to saline intrusion and to higher well water–pumping costs for both agriculture and urban users. To reverse this, SEWD is working in partnership with the U.S. Army Corps of Engineers and local water agencies on the Farmington Program.

This program's goal is to work with local landowners, businesses, growers, and ranchers to preserve the region's water supply. When surface water supplies are plentiful, the program will recharge the basin through in-lieu irrigation and partnerships with growers who rotate direct recharge activities with other land uses according to an agreement. Direct recharge facilities developed through the program contribute 11,000 acre-feet of water per year.

SEWD was formed in 1948 under the 1931 Water Conservation Act of the State of California. SEWD's mission is to ensure the proper management of the groundwater basin and to provide supplemental surface water supplies.

Today SEWD and SAWS are committed to Stockton's economic viability and quality of life by meeting the needs of residents and businesses. Looking to the future, SEWD's innovative strategies and programs will continue to keep up with the ever-growing demand for high quality water.

Above left: The MORE WATER Project will provide additional surface storage capacity and water supply reliability for the San Joaquin County region.
Above right: The Farmington Program begins to replenish the Eastern San Joaquin County Groundwater Basin.

Air Products and Chemicals, Inc.

This company serves a diversity of markets and supplies a wide array of products including merchant gases; tonnage gases, equipment, and energy; electronic and performance materials; and health care products. It develops and delivers all of its products and services with understanding, integrity, and passion.

Air Products and Chemicals, Inc., headquartered in Allentown, Pennsylvania, first invested in California in 1962 with a liquid hydrogen plant in Long Beach. It has since grown to become a leader in supplying hydrogen to refineries to make cleaner-burning fuels that meet the California Clean Fuel Standards, improving air quality by enhancing its customers' environmental performance, and helping to build the hydrogen economy of tomorrow. A Fortune 500 company, Air Products has annual revenues of $10 billion, operations in more than 40 countries, and 22,000 employees.

In Stockton, specifically, Air Products is the operator and co-owner with Atlantic Power Corporation of the Stockton CoGen Company, a solid fuels–fired power plant that produces steam and electricity for Corn Products International and for PG&E (Pacific Gas and Electric Company). One of the few coal-burning facilities in the state, the Stockton facility meets strict state emissions requirements and is actively involved with new programs and technologies that use renewable and previously wasted resources.

For example, Air Products—in cooperation with the Integrated Waste Management Board—developed a program to use shredded tires in the plant's fuel mix. Following stringent guidelines during supervised environmental testing, this program consumes as many as 2.5 million waste tires a year, helping to remove an eyesore and a fire hazard while providing the plant with an additional fuel supply. Efforts are also under way to investigate the use of biomass materials produced by the San Joaquin Valley agricultural industry for the production of steam and electrical power.

Environmental stewardship is not the only focus of Air Products in Stockton. Another source of pride concerns the safety of all employees and of the community. This is a number one priority for all Air Products facilities. Since opening in 1988, there has been only one lost day of work due to an injury. This outstanding record is attributable to employee commitment;

close partnerships with all local, state, and federal agencies; and frequent tours, training, and drills with emergency response teams.

Community participation is another of Air Products' commitments. Employees are encouraged to take part in community activities, including United Way, Junior Achievement, the Child Abuse Prevention Council of San Joaquin County, the Greater Stockton Emergency Food Bank, the Greater Stockton Chamber of Commerce's Manufacturing Industrial Distribution Roundtable, and a program in which experts work with teachers in local classrooms.

Additionally, the company has a local economic impact of $5 million to $6 million in payroll, taxes, and direct support to the local services and construction industries. Air Products and Chemicals, Inc. provides more information on its Web site (www.airproducts.com).

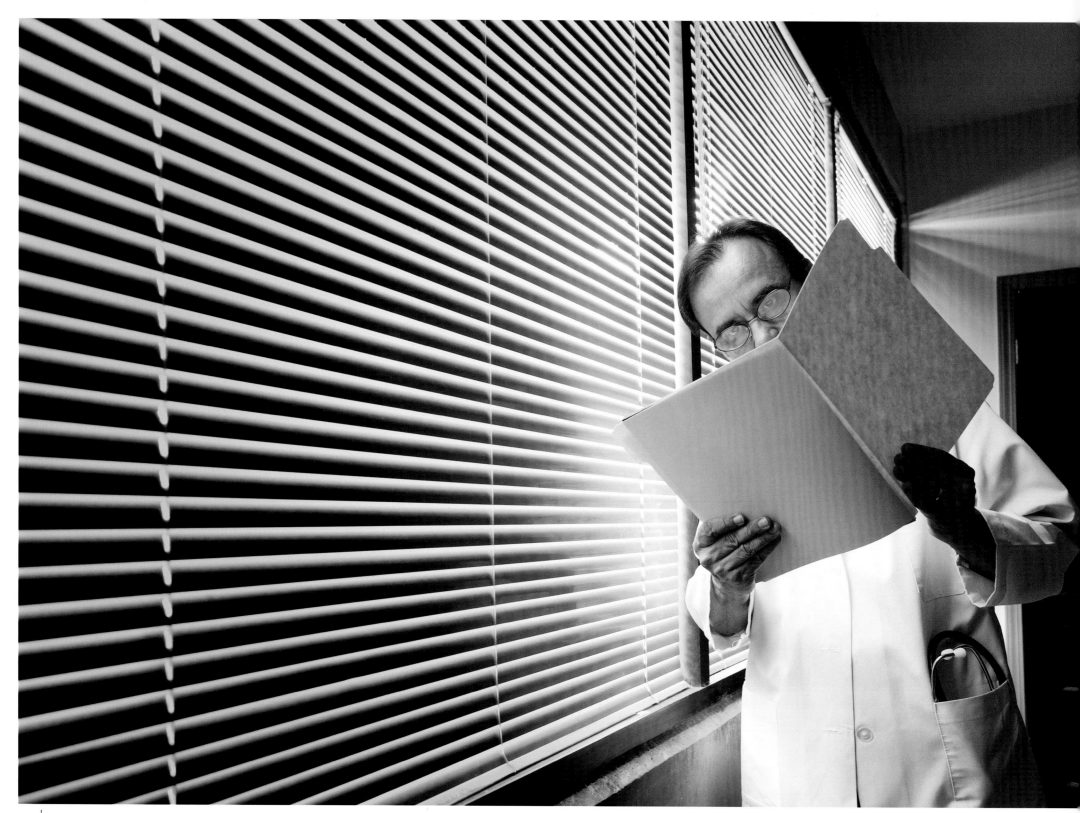

PROFILES OF COMPANIES AND ORGANIZATIONS
Health Care and Services

St. Joseph's Medical Center

Specializing in cardiovascular care, comprehensive cancer services, and women's and children's services, including neonatal intensive care, this large and popular full-service hospital is dedicated to the healing ministry of Jesus and bringing affordable health care to the communities it serves.

Above: St. Joseph's Medical Center is located at 1800 North California Street in Stockton, California. Its cornerstone was set on March 19, 1899.

St. Joseph's Medical Center, which opened in December 1899 as a 25-bed hospital supervised by the Dominican Sisters of San Rafael, now has 294 beds and employs over 2,400 people, including more than 400 physicians. Excelling particularly in cardiovascular care, women's and children's medicine, and cancer services, this nationally recognized medical center is the largest hospital and one of the largest private employers in San Joaquin County. Patients consistently choose it as their "most preferred hospital."

St. Joseph's Heart Center features three cardiac catheterization laboratories and two heart surgery suites, as well as a comprehensive diagnostic program. The center's range of care includes angioplasty and other intervention treatments, surgery, and cardiac rehabilitation. In 2008, HealthGrades awarded the center with the Cardiac Surgery Excellence award, and in fact, rated St. Joseph's the best in Northern California for cardiac surgery.

St. Joseph's Women & Children's Center helps bring more than 2,000 babies into the world each year. Prenatal and pediatric services see to the health and safety of infants and promote proper bonding between them and their parents. The Neonatal Intensive Care Nursery, a Level III facility, offers advanced care for infants, while the Pediatric Advanced Life Support (PALS) team offers child-friendly care at the hospital's 14-bed pediatric unit. The center's Welcome to Life classes ease the natural fears of parents-to-be and instill the confidence necessary to raise a happy and healthy child. Classes are open to the entire family.

St. Joseph's Cancer Center offers the area's most comprehensive cancer services with advanced medical technology and a wide range of support services for cancer patients and their families. A dedicated team of professionals that includes radiation therapists, dosimetrists, and physicists works under the direction of board-certified physicians to design specialized treatment plans to meet each individual patient's unique needs. St. Joseph's is the only cancer center in the area to meet the rigorous standards of clinical practice to be fully accredited by the American College of Surgeons Commission on Cancer and the Joint Commission.

St. Joseph's is so dedicated to the detection and treatment of breast cancer that it has implemented the Mobile Mammography Unit, a full-service mammography clinic on wheels, to bring early detection of breast cancer to 22 counties in the Central Valley and the surrounding foothills. The self-contained 18-wheeler visits churches, community centers, health fairs, community clinics, rural hospitals, and workplaces to reach underserved and underinsured women who may not otherwise have access to mammography screening.

St. Joseph's Cancer Navigator program helps patients negotiate the complex and often bewildering course of tests, treatments, and lifestyle changes following a positive biopsy. The free service provides breast cancer patients with educational, emotional, and logistical help and refers patients to agencies who meet their particular needs.

Specialists in the support team include an advanced oncology–certified nurse, a radiation specialist, and a social-support coordinator. The team is experienced in working with patients from a wide variety of linguistic and ethnic backgrounds, including Hispanic, Hmong, Laotian, and Thai.

Other community services include the Stockton Interfaith Caregiver Program, the Nurse Call Center, and St. Joseph's CareVan. The Stockton Interfaith Caregiver Program is a coalition of congregations and community agencies that help seniors improve their quality of life and maintain their independence. Volunteers help with shopping and other errands, offer respite care, and perform yard work and minor home maintenance. Sometimes the needed help is as simple as a friendly visit—and volunteers are happy to do that too. The Nurse Call Center provides free, around-the-clock, confidential answers to health care questions, a physician-referral service, and an audio library devoted to health care topics. St. Joseph's CareVan brings free health care to people who lack health insurance or access to primary care. Services range from treatment for acute problems such as fever and upper respiratory ailments, to help with chronic problems such as allergies and high blood pressure. The CareVan offers children's vaccinations as well.

The hospital also reaches out to the community by providing screening programs to detect skin, cervical, and prostate cancer and to increase public awareness of the dangers of diabetes.

Recognizing its responsibility to the environment, St. Joseph's environmental stewardship includes recycling paper, batteries, glass and plastic bottles, aluminum cans, printer cartridges, and green waste, among other products. Further, the hospital is a member of Ceres, a coalition of investors and environmental groups whose goal is to advance "sustainable prosperity"; Practice Greenhealth, which has awarded St. Joseph's with the Environmental Leadership award and Making Medicine Mercury Free award; and Health Care Without Harm, an international group dedicated to the delivery of environmentally responsible health care.

St. Joseph's Medical Center is a member of Catholic Healthcare West (CHW), a coalition of 42 hospitals and medical centers in California, Nevada, and Arizona. CHW is headquartered in San Francisco.

Above left: The beautiful stained-glass window in the lobby welcomes patients and visitors into St. Joseph's healing environment.
Above right: Compassionate care is provided to a patient in the hospital's Neonatal Intensive Care Unit (NICU).

Stockton Cardiology Medical Group

Using the most advanced procedures and medications available while drawing on their specialized knowledge, the physicians in this medical group deliver state-of-the-art cardiac care from four offices and five hospitals throughout the Stockton area.

Stockton Cardiology Medical Group (SCMG) and its predecessor group, which was established in the mid 1950s, have always provided the most advanced cardiovascular care. In 1976 the group's name was changed to its current full name—Stockton Cardiology Medical Group, Complete Heart Care, Inc. From establishing Stockton's first catheter laboratory in conjunction with the first coronary care unit to developing the heart center at St. Joseph's Medical Center in Stockton and founding the first in-office nuclear medicine laboratory in northern California, SCMG physicians take pride in being a part of a team that is known for excellent patient care and leading-edge procedures.

SCMG maintains offices in Stockton, Manteca, Tracy, and San Andreas (Calaveras County) and serves several hospitals, including St. Joseph's Medical Center, Dameron Hospital, Doctors Hospital of Manteca, Sutter Tracy Community Hospital, and Mark Twain St. Joseph's Hospital. A team of eight physicians share a health care philosophy and patient care principles that have guided the group from the start.

Among the group's unifying values are a dedication to the highest standards of cardiac care to diagnose and treat patients; respect for the dignity and value of all its patients, employees, and associates; continued growth in professional knowledge combined with a high standard of excellence and integrity for cardiac care in the community; and the promotion of the physical and mental well-being of all its employees and physicians.

A Full Spectrum of Services

SCMG offers a comprehensive heart and vascular program that includes cardiac risk factor assessment for the prevention of coronary artery disease (CAD), invasive and noninvasive cardiovascular evaluation, intervention for congenital heart disease, intervention for coronary artery disease, electrophysiology service, and peripheral vascular intervention.

Patient care begins with a cardiovascular consultation: the cardiologist obtains a detailed medical history from the patient, including risk factors, medications, and the current problem; performs a thorough exam of the heart and vascular system; and looks at all relevant test results. The physician may order additional tests after gathering and analyzing all of the necessary information.

Noninvasive Cardiovascular Diagnostics

Noninvasive cardiovascular diagnostic testing includes cardiac evaluation; coronary artery disease evaluation; and evaluation of carotid, renal, and peripheral vascular disease. Cardiac evaluation may require transthoracic two-dimensional echocardiography, which gives a moving picture of the heart using sound waves; nuclear medicine scans, using a camera to trace the heart's blood flow; an exercise test to determine how well the heart handles stress; and a 64-slice computed tomography (CT) scanner to obtain a noninvasive angiogram.

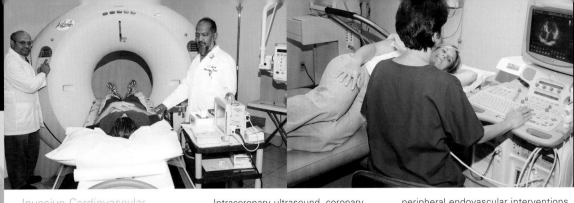

Coronary artery disease evaluation is made through the use of electrocardiography (a graphic record of electrical activity), echocardiography (ultrasound), and SPECT (single photon emission CT) myocardial perfusion imaging (injection of fluid to observe blood supply and circulation).

Evaluation of the carotid, renal, and peripheral vascular arteries is conducted through an ankle-brachial index, which measures blood pressure differences between the arms and the legs while the patient is at rest, and through a comprehensive vascular duplex ultrasound, which shows the physical structure of the patient's blood vessels.

Invasive Cardiovascular Evaluation

SCMG performs right heart catheterization, diagnostic angiography, intracoronary ultrasound, coronary Doppler flow, intracardiac echocardiography, and electrophysiology testing and arrhythmia management for patients who require invasive cardiovascular evaluation.

During right heart catheterization, electrocardiogram (EKG) patches attached to the patient's chest allow the heart's activity to be closely monitored. A catheter is then inserted through the neck or the groin area and passes into the right chambers of the heart, allowing the physician to record information about the heart's function.

During diagnostic angiography, an X-ray of an artery is used to diagnose blockages and other blood vessel abnormalities. A cardiologist guides a catheter into the artery and studies it while watching a monitor. Additional X-rays are taken after a dye is injected into the catheter, enabling the physician to visualize the blood vessels.

Intracoronary ultrasound, coronary Doppler flow, and intracardiac echocardiography are other forms of invasive evaluations involving sound waves that are used to evaluate the heart and determine treatment. Electrophysiology (EP) testing is used to precisely record the electrical activity within the heart and may be used to determine whether an extra electrical pathway exists.

Intervention for Coronary Artery Disease

Atherosclerosis can cause a reduction in blood flow to the heart muscle and can lead to chest pain (angina) or a heart attack. In addition to medications, percutaneous coronary intervention (PCI) is often performed. PCI involves dilating a narrowed artery with a small balloon and often placement of a medicated or bare-metal stent to help keep the artery open. In this way, PCI helps relieve symptoms and restores blood flow to the heart muscle.

Intervention for Peripheral Arterial Disease

Additional areas of special interest for SCMG are complex coronary and peripheral endovascular interventions, including carotid stenting and limb salvage procedures. Peripheral arterial disease (PAD) occurs when blood vessels outside the heart are diseased. It is reported that an estimated 20 million people in the United States have PAD, with an additional three to four million people who are untreated, often because of misdiagnosis.

PAD affects the arteries involved in peripheral circulation. In 2008 SCMG purchased a 64-slice CT scanner, which is the first noninvasive imaging technology that allows direct visualization of the coronary arteries and peripheral arteries. The scanner is capable of detecting atherosclerosis in its earliest stage, when treatment can be most effective. Patients who are diabetic, smoke, or suffer from hypertension are especially at risk for PAD.

Stockton Cardiology Medical Group will continue to expand in professional knowledge and to pursue a standard of excellence and integrity for cardiac care in San Joaquin County.

Above left: Dr. Lim monitors a patient during a cardiac stress test. Above center: Dr. Punjya and technologist Mohammed Masood perform a scan using a Toshiba 64-slice computed tomography (CT) scanner. Above right: Rebecca Dionne, cardiac sonographer, performs an echocardiography study.

Kaiser Permanente

This nonprofit organization is a leader in integrated health care, serving 8.7 million members in nine states and Washington, D.C. It is dedicated to providing high quality, affordable care with a unique team approach, a focus on prevention, and a commitment to caring for its communities.

Above: Kaiser Permanente invested $500 million to build the state-of-the-art Modesto Medical Center, which is located just east of Highway 99 in Modesto, California.

Kaiser Permanente, the country's largest integrated health care organization with nearly nine million members, first began serving California's Central Valley in 1984 when it opened the Stockton Medical Offices. Kaiser Permanente serves its Central Valley service area—which includes Stockton, Manteca, Modesto, Tracy, and other nearby communities—through Kaiser Permanente facilities, contracted inpatient medical centers, and community medical providers. In 2008 Kaiser Permanente added the new 670,000-square-foot Modesto Medical Center—the first major hospital to be built in the city in some 40 years—to its Central Valley facilities.

Kaiser Permanente strives to be the world leader in health care through high quality and affordable integrated care. The organization's hallmark is its ability to merge the key elements of health care—physicians, hospitals, home health care, ancillary care, and insurance—into a comprehensive, integrated delivery system. Kaiser Permanente believes that by creating an environment where these elements work together, it can deliver better quality health care to its consumers, who can receive preventive, routine, emergency, and hospital care from an organized system for a monthly fee.

A Connected Approach

Sharing information and expertise, Kaiser Permanente's physicians work together in teams to provide high quality care and service. The team approach creates a system that puts as many services as possible under one roof, delivering convenient health care and providing a simple process for referrals to specialists. To effectively supply highly specialized care, Kaiser Permanente concentrates its resources and expert physicians—who are well trained and well practiced in their specialties—at central locations.

As part of its team approach, Kaiser Permanente has implemented a groundbreaking, fully electronic medical record system. This program allows Kaiser Permanente professionals access to comprehensive patient information as well as to the latest best-practice research at the touch of a button to ensure patient safety and eliminate problems associated with incomplete, missing, or unreadable patient charts. The system provides physicians with full integration of inpatient, outpatient, and ancillary (radiology, laboratory, pharmacy) care to improve the quality of care delivered.

A Focus on Prevention

From its earliest roots, Kaiser Permanente has pioneered a focus on prevention in medical care in addition to treating sickness. Its broad benefit package encourages members to seek care before a medical problem becomes serious and costly.

To specifically address regional health needs, Kaiser Permanente reaches out to vulnerable populations to educate members about disease management and prevention, helping consumers to begin dealing with these conditions before they become severe.

Quality Physicians

Kaiser Permanente believes that good health care begins with the

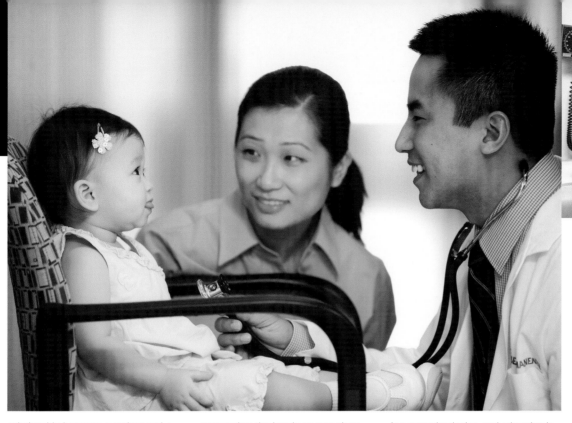

relationship between a patient and a personal physician or nurse practitioner from a primary care department, and it encourages all its members to choose a personal physician, who will provide and coordinate all medical services.

Kaiser Permanente in the Central Valley recruits quality physicians from across the country. The positive reputation of the Permanente Medical Group—the physician arm of Kaiser Permanente—greatly facilitates recruitment. Physicians are attracted to the hands-on care they are able to provide to their patients and to the integrated approach to care that allows them to make medical decisions based on the needs of their patients.

All Kaiser Permanente medical professionals undergo a rigorous, selective hiring process. Once they become a part of Kaiser Permanente, physicians and other caregivers receive ongoing training in their specialties as well as in general patient care, including cultural-sensitivity training, instruction in new technologies, and education in accepted best practices.

Healthy Communities
Kaiser Permanente demonstrates its core value of improving the health of its communities through a variety of programs, activities, and partnerships. Its Community Benefit program focuses on vulnerable populations, evidence-based medicine, education, and public policy. Kaiser Permanente annually awards more than $1.5 million in grants to the San Joaquin and Stanislaus counties' health care safety net—public hospitals and clinics that provide medical care to the uninsured. Additionally, it hosts the Neighbors in Health annual health fair—which provides screenings and services free of charge to uninsured and underinsured families—in Stockton, Manteca, and Modesto.

Kaiser Permanente doctors serve as Physician Ambassadors, visiting schools and other community organizations to deliver health messages. Additionally, the organization has a mobile health clinic that brings needed care into neighborhoods with populations that are at risk, and it supports national and local charitable organizations, such as United Way, the March of Dimes, and the American Cancer Society.

As a nonprofit health care organization, Kaiser Permanente considers its community efforts as part of its overall mission to improve health. It will continue to do so by delivering integrated care through a team approach that focuses on prevention.

Above left: Family practice physician James Redula, M.D., takes special care with his littlest patients. Above right: Young patients await their turn to have a physical examination from Felipe Dominguez, M.D., a longtime physician at the Stockton Medical Offices.

Gentiva Health Services

Delivering home care from 350 locations in 38 states, this exceptional provider of comprehensive home health care and related services continually strives to fulfill its mission, 'to improve quality of life and patient independence through the delivery of compassionate care and uncompromising service.'

Above left: Gentiva Health Services caregivers build a one-on-one relationship with their clients.
Above right: Among the many services offered by Gentiva are skilled nursing; neurorehabilitation services; durable medical and respiratory equipment; and other therapies and services.

The motto and mission of Gentiva Health Services employees is to "Seek Out and Serve Seniors" in the community. Gentiva, with operations in Stockton and across the country, knows the value of in-home health care. From skilled nursing assistance with everyday needs to physical therapy to high-technology procedures, the company's health care services are indispensable to thousand of patients

recovering from an illness or injury and to seniors who need help with basic activities. Delivered in familiar surroundings with loved ones nearby, Gentiva's services enhance the quality of life.

Widely regarded as the industry leader in home health care based on its range and scope of nationwide services, Gentiva has provided outstanding comprehensive services and care since 1971, and locally in the Stockton area since 1983. The company offers nursing, physical, occupational, and speech therapy; social work; nutrition; disease-management education; help with daily living activities; infusion therapy; and more.

Home health care offers unprecedented career opportunities and challenges. Gentiva caregivers enjoy a one-on-one relationship with patients, enabling them to recover quickly and play an active role in their own treatment. This type of care makes a positive difference in the lives of patients and family members, as well as Gentiva clinicians.

Kristi Halva, branch director for Gentiva in Stockton, emphasizes Gentiva team

members' devotion to serving senior citizens. "We want to respond to the needs of the local population as a small business by reflecting the health care concerns and wants of our local community," she says, "while also delivering the benefits and resources afforded by a large company. Many of the company's innovative programs, for which our staff receives specialized training, are just what seniors need to continue living at home independently."

Employees at Gentiva recognized needs in the community related to an increasing number of falls among seniors and a need for a specialized program. From this, Gentiva developed a comprehensive balance program that evaluates and treats balance dysfunctions to help prevent falls and resulting injuries. Called Gentiva Safe Strides®, this program is offered locally to the Stockton community. In addition to Gentiva Safe Strides are specialty programs offered nationally, including Gentiva Orthopedics, Gentiva Cardiopulmonary, and Neurorehabilitation.

Gentiva Health Services believes its foundation of excellence is rooted

in the individuals who deliver the company's services. The benefits of working for Gentiva include medical, dental, vision, life, and disability insurance; retirement savings plans and stock purchase plans; tuition assistance; superior training; and free continuing education credits through Gentiva University.

PROFILES OF COMPANIES AND ORGANIZATIONS
Hospitality

Hilton Stockton

Conveniently located in the center of Stockton, this newly remodeled full-service hotel offers well-appointed guest rooms, an array of amenities, and first-rate meeting facilities for both business and leisure travelers. Its dedicated staff is committed to meeting and exceeding the needs of each of its guests.

PACIFICA
C O M P A N I E S
HOTEL PROJECT – STOCKTON, CA.

HOTEL FACADE & ENTRIES

DARRALL DESIGN CONSULTANTS
11444 W. OLYMPIC BLVD. SUITE 120
WEST LOS ANGELES, CA. 90064-1549 USA
310-478-1768   FAX 310-478-1826
E-MAIL: dardescon@earthlink.net

Full-Service Amenities

Guests at the Hilton Stockton enjoy an outdoor swimming pool and whirlpool spa, a fitness center with both cardiovascular and strength-training equipment, and complimentary parking. Located within the hotel is the Atrium Restaurant, featuring cooked-to-order entrees and the best of California cuisine. Room service is available all day, and the sports-themed cocktail lounge offers a relaxing atmosphere.

With 13,000 square feet of meeting space, the hotel is a popular venue for business and social events. These facilities can accommodate from 10 to 500 people and include the Delta Ballroom and 10 additional conference rooms. The hotel's meeting spaces offer wireless high-speed Internet access and audiovisual equipment. The hotel's catering and event-planning services help to make any kind of meeting or gathering a success.

An Array of Local Attractions

Situated in the heart of the city, the Hilton Stockton provides its guests with an easily accessible location

Above: The contemporary Hilton Stockton is centrally located in northern California, in close proximity to downtown Stockton's business center and to many of the region's best attractions, entertainment venues, and recreational areas.

The Hilton Stockton takes pride in its friendly and attentive team, which strives to provide the best possible service for every visitor. Each of the hotel's newly remodeled guest rooms offers comfort and convenience. Its desirable location near Interstate 5 makes it a top choice for both business and leisure travelers.

Delivering Comfort and Convenience

The Hilton Stockton has 198 new guest rooms, with an earth-toned interior design that creates a calming, relaxed ambience. Each well-appointed guest room has been created to provide a productive and comfortable stay. Rooms include a two-line telephone with voice mail, high-speed Internet access, numerous premium television channels, coffeemakers, an iron and ironing board, and a hairdryer. The hotel's luxury guest suites offer additional features such as a separate bedroom, a living and dining area, and a balcony for relaxing.

that is within minutes of some of Stockton's most popular dining, shopping, and recreational attractions, from sports venues, theaters, and nightclubs to museums and science centers. Sports enthusiasts will enjoy the Reserve at Spanos Park, a golf course designed by noted golf course architect Andy Raugust;

the Stockton 99 Speedway, which hosts Nascar competitions; and the Stockton Arena, home of the Stockton Thunder hockey team, the Stockton Lightning football team, and the California Cougars soccer team. The San Joaquin Delta offers hotel guests more than 1,000 miles of waterways for outdoor recreation.

Performing and visual arts abound in Stockton. The San Joaquin Delta College and the University of the Pacific and its Conservatory of Music, Brubeck Institute, and Theatre Arts department host concerts, music festivals, plays, and other events. Hotel guests will enjoy the festivals, concerts, shows, and Broadway productions held at the Weber Point Events Center, the Stockton Civic Theatre, and the historic Bob Hope Theatre. The Hilton Stockton is also close to the Haggin Museum, the

Children's Museum of Stockton, the George H. Clever Planetarium at San Joaquin Delta College, and Earth Science Center.

The full-service Hilton Stockton is committed to providing each of its visitors with a comfortable stay. With its spacious guest rooms, many amenities, flexible meeting space, and proximity to a wide range of local attractions, it will continue to meet and exceed the needs of its guests.

Left: Guests at the Hilton Stockton can stroll along a scenic waterway canal in front of the hotel. Above right: The hotel's Delta Ballroom is one of the most popular wedding locations in the Stockton area, offering elegant decor, delicious food, and a pleasant ambience. The hotel's 13,000 square feet of flexible meeting space can accommodate gatherings of almost any size.

Both pages: The beautiful waterfront Sheraton Stockton Hotel at Regent Pointe offers gorgeous views and easy access to the marina, and is conveniently located next to the Stockton Arena. The hotel's unique shape maximizes views from the rooms.

Conveniently located in the heart of Stockton, the elegant Sheraton Stockton Hotel at Regent Pointe stands on the water's edge alongside the city's beautiful Delta Waterway. The delta offers an abundance of recreational activities and may be the perfect place for hotel guests to relax in one of nature's loveliest settings.

The Sheraton Stockton offers well-appointed guest rooms and suites, a wide range of amenities, and meeting facilities that accommodate 50 to 400 people in comfortable settings with views of the delta. As the anchor of the Regent Pointe development, this modern, seven-story hotel is conveniently surrounded by many attractions and is within walking distance of shops, restaurants, and entertainment venues. Just minutes away are the multimillion-dollar Stockton Arena, Weber Point Events Center and Banner Island Ballpark, the Bob Hope Theatre, the Stockton Cineplex Plaza, and the Stockton Marina.

The hotel features a nautical theme that reflects a coastal lifestyle and brings in the ambience of the marina. The interior decor evokes a yachting tradition with a refreshing color palette of blue and white, textures of natural canvas and striped fabrics, and nickel and chrome fittings.

All of the hotel's 179 guest rooms and suites feature Sheraton Sweet Sleeper beds for a supremely comfortable night's sleep; a city or waterfront view; a 32-inch plasma television with in-room movies; coffeemaker and premium coffee and tea; and an array of bath products. Guest rooms provide large work desks and telephones with voice mail, and high-speed Internet access is available.

The hotel also provides a fully equipped fitness center featuring weight machines and cardiovascular equipment, an outdoor swimming pool for recreation and relaxation, and a whirlpool spa. Guests can enjoy the convenience of concierge service, laundry service, and room service. At the hotel's dining venue, the Hippo Bar and Restaurant, the cuisine includes a tapas menu and a full cocktails menu to satisfy the most discerning tastes.

Meetings and events at the Sheraton Stockton are well executed by an experienced team of meeting planners and chefs. Up to 400 people can be seated in the ballroom or conference room, or an event can be held on the outdoor lawn. The staff can make arrangements that embrace every event detail and excels in providing custom-designed menus, organizing audiovisual services, and filling special requests to contribute to the success of an event.

With its inviting guest rooms and suites, full amenities, and ample space for hosting family and business events of all kinds, the Sheraton Stockton Hotel at Regent Pointe offers a setting for a productive and relaxing sojourn.

PROFILES OF COMPANIES AND ORGANIZATIONS
Legal Services

Neumiller & Beardslee

Founded in 1903, this outstanding law firm has grown and changed along with the Stockton community, representing many of the area's largest businesses, institutions, and government agencies while expertly serving the needs of individual clients.

"To provide high quality legal services and maintain a high level of service to clients and the community" has been the goal of Neumiller & Beardslee for more than a century. The firm is proud of its history—which is intricately tied to the growth and development of Stockton and the San Joaquin area—and equally proud of the team of lawyers who have continually responded to the needs of the community by representing individuals, small and large businesses, professional groups, nonprofit organizations, and governmental agencies.

The Original Partnership

Already one of California's larger cities, turn-of-the-century Stockton was growing rapidly, serving as a transportation hub and as a center for agricultural production and agricultural equipment manufacturing. It was in this setting and era that Stockton lawyers Arthur H. Ashley and Charles L. Neumiller met.

Ashley was the district attorney of San Joaquin County at the time, and Neumiller became a member of his staff. In 1902, when Ashley's four-year term ended, the men decided to enter into a business partnership. The following year they leased space in the New Salz Building across from the courthouse, with their rent payable in gold, and began working for important clients such as the Benjamin Holt Company, which Neumiller had helped form.

Ashley opened a practice on his own in 1910, while Neumiller continued to practice law with various associates. Among them was George A. Ditz, who joined Neumiller in 1913 and became a partner two years later.

Expanding with the City

The firm of Neumiller & Ditz was a part of many important events that shaped Stockton between 1913 and 1928. The firm handled the litigation between Holt Manufacturing Company and C. L. Best Tractor Company, for instance, which culminated in the creation of the Caterpillar Tractor Company, and the firm also opened the door for the Western Pacific Railroad to come to town.

Neumiller's nephew Irving L. Neumiller joined the firm in 1923 and became a partner in 1925. He was a well-known trial lawyer, and founded the firm's trial practice. Robert L. Beardslee joined the firm in 1930 and became a partner in 1941. He continued the firm's prominence in the Stockton legal community, counseling important local businesses such as the State Savings and Loan Association, Holt Brothers, Hickenbotham Brothers, and the Pacific Storage Company. He remained in practice for a remarkable 69 years.

Beardslee, Ditz, and Irving Neumiller formed the firm's core group of attorneys until 1945, when the firm mushroomed to keep pace with Stockton's thriving economy during the postwar boom.

Water Works and Land Development Successes

The numerous public works projects to which the firm has lent its expertise include the New Melones Dam,

the last major dam built in California; the Stockton East Water District treatment plant, an important supplier of water; and the Altamont Commuter Express rail service between Stockton and Silicon Valley. The firm's work for local water agencies flowed into more projects for cities, public districts, transportation agencies, and the Port of Stockton today.

In the late 1960s the firm began to represent residential and commercial real estate developers in the areas of land development, subdivision development, and construction. The hundreds of subdivisions whose developers the firm has helped include Lincoln Village West, Quail Lakes, Venetian Village and Venetian Bridges, Spanos Park East and West, Lakeshore Village, Brookside Estates, University Park, and Mountain House.

The firm's name has included various attorneys through the years, including Neumiller, Beardslee, Diehl, Siegert, Glahn, Shephard, and Greene in 1966. The name was simplified in 1975 to Neumiller & Beardslee, and was incorporated as such in 1981.

Legal Expertise and Community Investment

Today Neumiller & Beardslee is one of the area's largest law firms, employing more than 24 attorneys and more than 20 members of legal staff. The firm carries on with its tradition of representing clients who play a prominent role in the Stockton area, including numerous cities, special districts, and other governmental agencies, as well as financial institutions, real estate developers, health care organizations, religious organizations and churches, corporations, and local wineries.

Neumiller & Beardslee's practice areas include real estate, land use, water law, environmental law, employment law, health care law, intellectual property and information technology law, banking law, litigation, public agency law, church law, transportation law, business law, bankruptcy law, tax law, public and private financings, probate, and estate planning.

In addition to the practice of law, Neumiller & Beardslee remains deeply involved in the community through the volunteer efforts of its attorneys and

staff, many of whom serve on the boards of various civic and nonprofit organizations, are actively involved in local charities, and donate their time to a wide variety of local causes. As well as their involvement with community service, a number of attorneys also serve on boards of regional concern.

Neumiller & Beardslee's diverse and progressive practice areas combined with its commitment to the community have made the firm a notable part of Stockton's history, and will help make it part of Stockton's future.

Left: Shown here on the rooftop of Neumiller & Beardslee's office overlooking Stockton's waterfront are Neumiller & Beardslee attorneys, from left, (front row) Mike McGrew, Paul Balestracci, Dan Schroeder, Cliff Stevens, Jim Dyke, and Chris Greene; (second row) Saroya Leonardini, Duncan McPherson, Tom Shephard, John Stovall, Mia Brown, and Rudy Bilawski; (third row) Tony Despotes, Karen Bensch, DeeAnne Gillick, Lisa Blanco-Jimenez, Monica Streeter, and Rod Attebery; (fourth row) Jim Nuss, Dan Truax, and Michael Tener; and (back row) Suzanne Kennedy, Nathan McGuire, and Jennifer Alves.

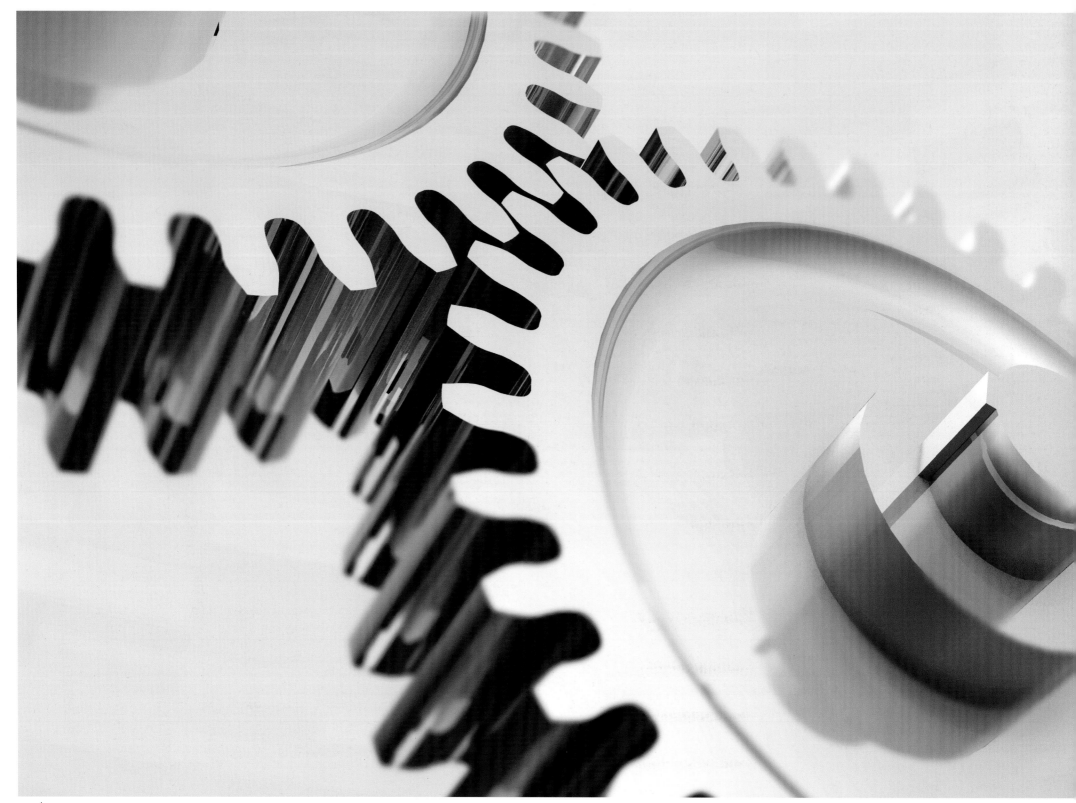

PROFILES OF COMPANIES AND ORGANIZATIONS
Manufacturing and Distribution

Holt of California

Since 1931 this equipment dealer has been noted for 'helping customers move the earth, build communities, and feed the world.' An authorized Caterpillar dealer, Holt of California serves 16 counties in central northern California.

In 1904 Benjamin Holt tested a steam-powered machine that moved on self-laying tracks instead of wheels; he called this invention "Caterpillar." Later in the early 1900s, the Marysville Tractor & Equipment Company and Holt Bros. were formed as Caterpillar dealers to cover regions of northern California. In 1963 Marysville Tractor & Equipment Company changed its name to Tenco Tractor, and finally in 1999 the two merged to become what is known today as Holt of California.

The invention of Benjamin Holt led to today's Fortune 100 company Caterpillar Inc., headquartered in Peoria, Illinois, with approximately 180 authorized dealerships worldwide. Holt of California is one of those authorized Caterpillar equipment dealers, serving 16 counties in central northern California. Holt of California sells, services, and rents Caterpillar-manufactured equipment to a variety of customers throughout its five marketing divisions—Earthmoving, Agriculture, Power Systems, Material Handling, and The Cat Rental Store.

Right: The Haggin Museum's Holt Memorial Hall features an esteemed gallery that documents Stockton's contributions to industrial history, and its exhibits include a Holt 75 Caterpillar track-type tractor, which was developed in Stockton.

HOLT of California

THEN ... A test drive of the track-type wheel on Holt Steam Tractor No. 77

Now ... Caterpillar continues to improve on an original concept. Caterpillar's track-type tractor is the No. 1 seller in the world.

FOREVER ... Holt '75' on display in The Haggin Museum's Holt Memorial Hall

For over 75 years we've been helping customers move the earth, build communities and feed the world. Then and now our best asset is our customers and we work hard each day to exceed their expectations.

1 (800) 347-4658   Serving Central Northern California   www.holtca.com

dedicated to educating future leaders on the technology of tomorrow. Implementing Caterpillar's ThinkBIG program, Holt of California offers motivated candidates an opportunity to become Caterpillar Dealer Service Technicians. Together with Caterpillar Inc., with other Caterpillar dealers, and San Joaquin Delta College, this program develops highly skilled professionals that are in demand to work on some of the world's most advanced pieces of equipment.

Customers and communities are two of the driving forces behind Holt of California. With its commitment to quality and service, Holt of California is a leading equipment supplier in central northern California. More than 75 years of history, a solid reputation, and a strong future ahead give Holt of California the power to change the face of the industrial equipment industry.

Breaking new ground is not the only focus of Holt of California. The company also promotes its six core values and challenges all employees to strive to live up to these core values daily. Holt of California's goal is to bring valuable solutions to its customers by continually exceeding their expectations and by adapting to their changing needs.

In addition to serving its customers' current needs, Holt of California is

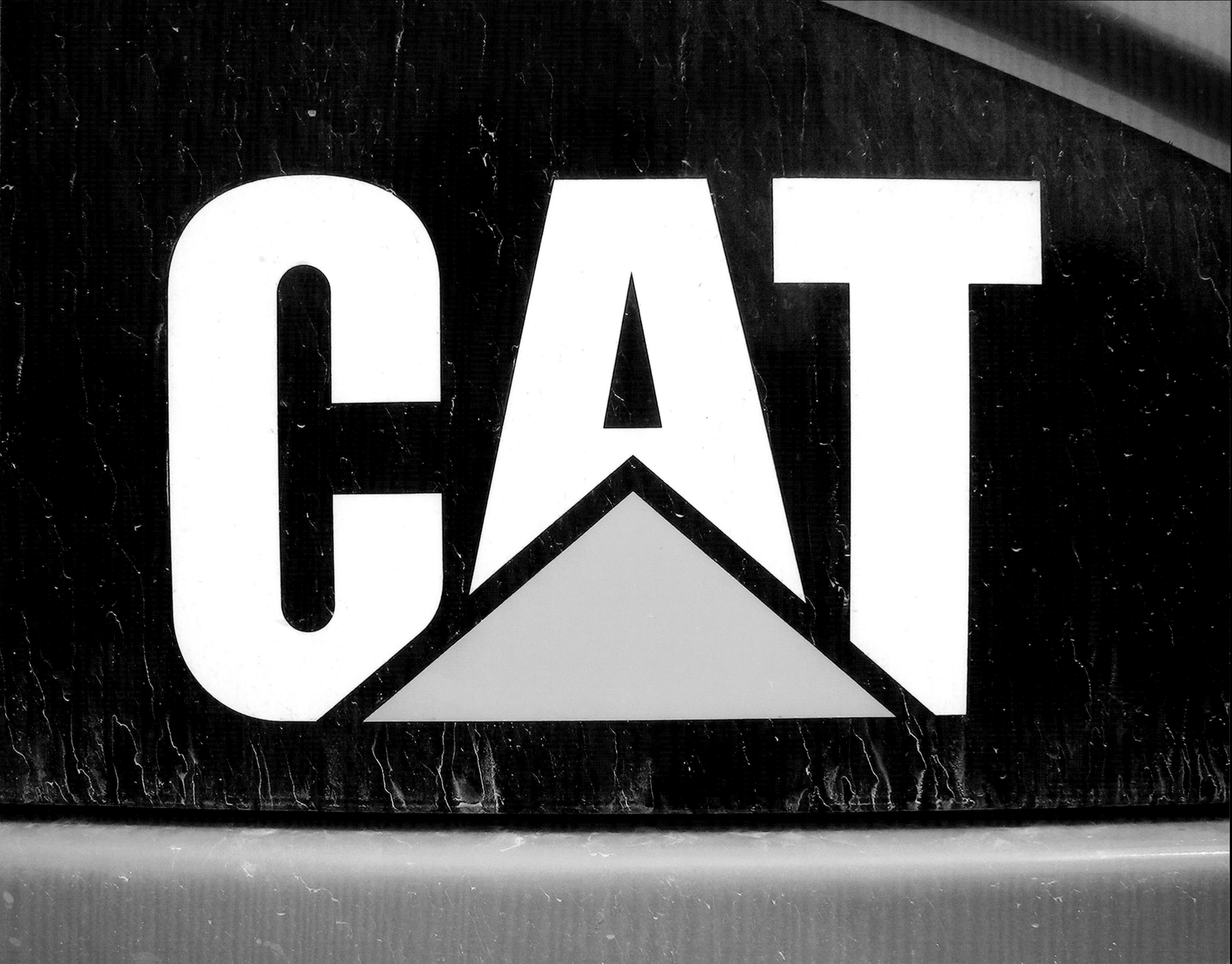
CAT

PROFILES OF COMPANIES AND ORGANIZATIONS
Professional and Business Services

Iacopi, Lenz & Company

This resourceful and innovative accounting firm provides comprehensive services in a timely manner to clients in a wide range of industries. Since 1978 it has remained dedicated to delivering the highest quality, personal service to its clients as well as giving back to its community.

Professional Services

Located in Stockton, Iacopi, Lenz & Company serves both individual and business clients. It is dedicated to delivering the highest quality service and prides itself on doing so in a timely manner. As a relatively small firm, it is able to offer personal service. Its diverse clientele includes the following industries and professionals: farmers, food processors, grocery stores, restaurants, manufacturers, trucking companies, developers, nonprofit organizations, educational institutions, professional athletes, physicians, engineers, and attorneys.

Iacopi, Lenz & Company takes a proactive approach to taxes and tax services by gaining an understanding of each client's unique needs. The firm uses its knowledge of current tax legislation to provide tax planning, identifying ways its clients may reduce their current and future tax liabilities. It efficiently and accurately prepares tax returns for a variety of entities, from individuals, partnerships, and corporations to trusts and estates. The firm also provides experienced representation for its clients before federal and state tax agencies.

Above: The staff of Iacopi, Lenz & Company is composed of seasoned professionals dedicated to creating the best possible outcomes for their clients.

In 1978 John T. Iacopi started the accounting firm of Iacopi and Fox. The firm experienced steady growth, and in 1980 Iacopi became the sole owner. Susan H. Lenz, who joined the firm in 1978, became a partner in 1982, and the firm became known as Iacopi & Lenz. In 2001 Michael S. Butler, who joined the firm in 1980, and Michael D. Luis, who joined the firm in 1991, each attained the position of principal of the firm. Known today as Iacopi, Lenz & Company—the firm has grown beyond its original four employees to a staff of 26 dedicated associates, including 17 certified public accountants. With a 30-year anniversary celebration in 2008, the firm meets the needs of its clients through general practice accounting, income tax preparation, and business consulting.

Through its extensive accounting services, the firm delivers meaningful, well-organized financial information accurately and promptly, including audits, reviews, and compilations as well as bookkeeping, QuickBooks support, and financial statement preparation.

Iacopi, Lenz & Company also offers consulting services to its business clients, helping them choose the type of entity—corporation, sole proprietorship, limited liability company/partnership, or another form—that will provide the greatest business advantage. It also provides guidance to clients who are considering acquiring, selling, or merging a business or who are planning for business succession. The firm also provides litigation support, forensic accounting, expert witness testimony, and wealth transfer and estate planning services.

The staff at Iacopi, Lenz & Company, which includes Certified Valuation Analysts, performs business appraisal services for business planning, gifting, marital dissolutions, and litigation purposes.

A Valuable, Informative Resource

Iacopi, Lenz & Company is dedicated to providing professional accounting services and is passionate about its commitment to the firm's clients. Iacopi, Lenz & Company makes itself available to clients seven days a week. As part of its efforts to offer superior service and support, it has developed a Web site (www.iacopi.com) that serves as a helpful resource for financial and accounting information. The site includes financial tools, such as interactive calculators, and informative articles in its online newsletter.

Dedicated Associates

Iacopi, Lenz & Company maintains an environmentally conscious office that is committed to its profession and the community. The firm's clients appreciate the continuity and longevity of its staff in that numerous staff members have been with the firm 20 years or longer. Members of the firm have contributed to the accounting industry by writing articles for accounting publications, speaking at professional seminars and forums, and chairing committees of professional organizations. A member of the firm's staff, Constance D. Logan, a Certified Public Accountant and an attorney, serves as a member of the IRS Commissioner Information Reporting Program Advisory Committee in Washington, D.C. She also served as a law clerk in the Ninth Circuit Federal Court of Appeals.

Employees of the firm also serve as board members and officers for charitable organizations and they are proud of their involvement in civic, educational, and community organizations.

Through its more than 30 years in business, Iacopi, Lenz & Company has continued to expand and deliver a wide range of accounting services. As it celebrates this success, the firm looks to continue to meet the needs of its clients and its community.

Above left: Iacopi, Lenz & Company corporate offices are located at 3031 West March Lane in Stockton, California. Above right: Company principals include (left to right): Michael S. Butler, Susan H. Lenz, John T. Iacopi, and Michael D. Luis.

PROFILES OF COMPANIES AND ORGANIZATIONS
Real Estate, Construction, and Development

A. G. Spanos Companies

For Alex G. Spanos, a dream and hard work led to a successful construction and development company. A leading builder of multifamily properties, commercial buildings, and master-planned communities in the United States, the company brings quality and integrity to all of its impressive projects.

Right: Proudly established and still headquartered in Stockton, California, A. G. Spanos Companies is a builder of award-winning projects as well as great communities. Most recently, the company was honored with two Aurora awards for its development of the European-inspired 387-unit Cheval Apartment urban complex in Houston, Texas. This prestigious award is given by the Southeast Building Conference. Overall, A. G. Spanos has earned its reputation for integrity, high quality, and excellence over its 50 years of operation in the state and across the nation.

In 1960 Alex G. Spanos founded A. G. Spanos Construction Co. and built his first apartment building. Since then the company, now called A. G. Spanos Companies, has developed living communities, commercial projects, and mixed-use developments. A family-run business, it has built over 400 developments nationwide, including more than 120,000 apartment units and over two million square feet of office space. The company is headquartered in Stockton, California, and operates regional offices in Florida, Georgia, Nevada, Texas, Kansas, Colorado, Arizona, North Carolina, and northern and southern California.

A. G. Spanos's master-planned communities set new standards for resort-style living, with spacious apartments, landscaping, fitness centers, swimming pools, spas, and other amenities. For example, in Vacaville, California, residents at the conveniently located North Pointe Apartments enjoy the gracious lifestyle and amenities that typify an A. G. Spanos community. The gated-access complex offers features such as tile flooring, full-length mirrors, special bathroom lighting, a state-of-the-art fitness center, and more. Sycamore Terrace in Sacramento provides varied floor plans and is close to downtown.

Sharing the Wealth

Born in Stockton in 1923, Spanos founded his company in his hometown, where he maintains his residence. He believes in giving back to the community, as he noted in his autobiography, *Sharing the Wealth: My Story*, published in 2002.

In Stockton, Spanos was the principal donor for the renovation of the Bob Hope Theatre, named for his good friend, and for the University of the Pacific's Faye Spanos Concert Hall, named for his wife of 60 years. Spanos also has donated to many local arts and theater groups.

He has given time and money to many organizations in Stockton and elsewhere, including United Way, the YMCA, Starlight Starbright Children's Foundation, sports teams, homeless shelters, and relief organizations. Spanos owns the San Diego Chargers football team, and he and San Diego football fans contributed generously to tsunami relief for southeast Asia in 2004. Spanos has aided a number of hospitals, including St. Joseph's and Dameron hospitals in Stockton, as well as Sacramento's Mercy General Hospital, which named its heart center for him.

Spanos has contributed to many colleges, including the University of the Pacific; California State University, Sacramento; California Polytechnic Institute, San Luis Obispo; and the University of California, Berkeley. In Stockton, he donated to St. Mary's High School, Samuel Hancock School, and Lincoln High School and established scholarships in the school districts.

With more than 600 employees, A. G. Spanos Companies will continue to build housing communities and commercial structures across the nation.

Escalon at Canyon Creek, an A. G. Spanos development in Austin, Texas

PROFILES OF COMPANIES AND ORGANIZATIONS
Transportation and Logistics

Port of Stockton

A strategic link for the distribution of goods, this 2,000-acre transportation center provides a direct route to the Pacific Ocean, port cities worldwide, and all U.S. markets. The port offers a 35-foot deepwater channel, first-rate cargo handling and warehousing, and immediate access for shipping by highway, rail, and air.

Centrally located 75 nautical miles due east of the Golden Gate Bridge, at the intersection of four major highways, two transcontinental railroads, and a regional airport, the Port of Stockton sits in the fertile San Joaquin Valley at the point where the San Joaquin River and the Stockton deepwater ship channel meet. This opportune geographic position and the port's first-rate handling services and warehouse storage enable the 2,000-acre transportation center to provide optimal service to companies shipping and storing cargo. The port is a designated Foreign Trade Zone, giving importers and exporters advantages in delayed payments or exemption from U.S. Customs duties.

The Port of Stockton's activities involve the shipments of many industries that positively impact the economy of California. Liquid fertilizer and sulphur are two important commodities due to the volume processed and the importance of their role in the agricultural businesses that operate throughout the San Joaquin Valley. Since the start of the new millennium, the port's largest import is cement and its largest export is California bagged rice.

Creating the Deepwater Channel

The discovery of gold in northern California in the mid 1800s turned the Stockton channel into a riverboat landing that served the mining industry. By the 1890s the city of Stockton had become a thriving transportation and commercial center. Flour mills, grain elevators, carriage and wagon factories, iron foundries, and shipyards surrounded the channel and its tributaries. By the end of the 19th century, agriculture was booming throughout California's Central Valley, and inventions such as advanced farming equipment and improved tools were being produced by local companies, making Stockton one of the state's major industrialized cities.

In 1929 the U.S. Congress approved federal funding to deepen the San Joaquin River at Stockton after extensive lobbying by leaders in the agriculturally rich Central Valley. These pioneers convinced authorities that a port that would enable the valley to be connected with the rest of the world was vital to the future of Stockton and the many communities growing nearby. The first contracts for dredging the channel were awarded in 1930.

Three factors were pivotal to the dredging of the channel and the creation of the deepwater port: the Fair Trade law was passed in California in 1931—an important step toward creating the port district; a unified rail service was created by agreement between the City of Stockton and three

transcontinental railroads; and the Belt Line Railroad was installed in 1932.

When the Port of Stockton officially opened in 1933 it had a depth of 26 feet to accommodate the ocean-going ships of the day, and it was the first inland seaport in California. In 1987 completion of a second dredging project brought the channel to its present 35-foot depth. Vessels up to 55,000 tons, as well as some 60,000-ton, wide-beam vessels, can use the channel with full loads; there is no width restriction for vessels. The channel accommodates ships up to 900 feet in length. The well-known Delta, created by the merging of several rivers and many man-made channels, continues to shape the economy of the city of Stockton, its port, and its surrounding communities.

Services and Facilities

The Port of Stockton's diversified transportation services encompass a 2,000-acre operating area and offer facilities and equipment to handle break-bulk and container cargoes by land or by sea. This includes berthing space for 15 vessels, 1.1 million square feet of dockside transit shed and shipside rail trackage, and 7.7 million square feet of warehousing for both dry and liquid bulk materials and general cargo, including steel. Warehouses are served by Union Pacific and Burlington Northern Santa Fe Railway complemented by two loop railroads for unit trains and for consolidating rail shipments.

The Port of Stockton is well suited for handling heavy steel and project cargoes, with its overland transportation connections and its more than

30 acres of paved surface that facilitate assembly and prestaging. For example, the port attracts industrial-development projects that require transport by water for delivering raw or finished materials and goods.

The port offers three traveling, multi-purpose, 30-ton bridge cranes, which can handle dry bulk import cargoes as well as containers and steel products. In addition, floating cranes and mobile truck cranes are available. Cargo can be transferred directly from vessels to truck, rail, dockside storage, and conveyor. Two bulk loading towers are used to load all types of export bulk material—including coal, petroleum coke, ores, clay, and sulfur.

The Port of Stockton provides information about its facilities and services on its Web site (www.portofstockton.com).

All of the port's services are directed by experienced staff members through one administrative complex, providing flexibility and efficiency for customers. The port publishes tariffs, stevedores cargoes, assigns berths, supervises cargo activity, and provides shipping documentation, accounting, and rate quotations.

The Port of Stockton is a hands-on organization whose activities include marketing, traffic handling, property management, warehousing, distribution, data processing, and security services for its customers. The port has its own Police Department, staffed by professional police officers and trained police dogs. The port police patrol 24 hours a day, seven days a week.

Top left: The Port of Stockton is served by more than 200 truck companies including all of the major transcontinental carriers. Top center and top right: Ships' gear handles steel products and containers as well as dry bulk cargo. Above right: The year 2008 marks the 75th anniversary of the Port of Stockton.

San Joaquin Regional Transit District

San Joaquin County's regional transit provider operates routes within the Stockton metropolitan area and connects the cities and rural communities with its Intercity, Interregional, and Dial-A-Ride services. Its buses transport riders to school, work, shopping venues, and recreational destinations.

The San Joaquin Regional Transit District (RTD) began in 1965 as the Stockton Metropolitan Transit District (SMTD), providing public bus service to the city of Stockton. In 1994 the SMTD service area was expanded to include all of San Joaquin County, and the district's name was changed to San Joaquin Regional Transit District.

RTD is the regional transit provider for Stockton and San Joaquin County. RTD operates 365 days a year, providing fixed-route service to the Stockton metropolitan area, including

Bus Rapid Transit service and trolley routes. RTD Interregional Commuter routes connect Stockton to Sacramento, the Bay Area, and the Dublin/Pleasanton Bay Area Rapid Transit (BART) station. RTD intercity and rural routes connect Stockton, Lodi, Tracy, Manteca, Ripon, Lathrop, and the unincorporated communities of San Joaquin County. Dial-A-Ride buses provide door-to-door service in Stockton and countywide.

Total annual ridership for fiscal year 2007 was just under four million trips. As of 2008 RTD had more than 325

administrative, maintenance, and transportation employees. RTD has used diesel-electric hybrid buses since 2004. In 2008 hybrid buses composed 30 percent of RTD's full-size Metro fleet. Metro Express—RTD's Bus Rapid Transit service—is a limited-stop express bus service connecting north Stockton with downtown Stockton, including stops that serve shopping centers, San Joaquin Delta College, and the University of the Pacific. RTD will expand its Bus Rapid Transit service as Stockton continues to develop.

The RTD Downtown Transit Center (DTC) was completed in 2006. Nearly all RTD routes connect at the DTC, which has two passenger boarding platforms with 20 sheltered, off-street bus stops. The DTC building incorporates the facades of three historic buildings on its front elevation. The DTC first floor has a waiting area, public restrooms, customer service center, police satellite station, boardroom, and retail space. RTD administrative offices occupy the rest of the building. On average, more than 6,000 people use the DTC each weekday. In 2008 RTD also operated two other

maintenance and operations facilities. Future plans include the consolidation of RTD operations facilities.

The San Joaquin Regional Transit District is an active community partner, and it remains committed to its primary mission—providing a safe, reliable, and efficient transportation system for Stockton and San Joaquin County. Its vision is to be the transportation service of choice for the customers it serves.

Left: Metro Express is one of the ways in which San Joaquin RTD is keeping pace with Stockton's progressive development.

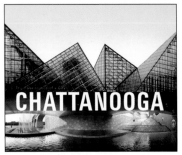

Jack Cherbo, Cherbo Publishing Group president and CEO, has been breaking new ground in the sponsored publishing business for more than 40 years.

"Previously, the cost of creating a handsome book for business developments or commemorative occasions fell directly on the sponsoring organization," Cherbo says. "My company pioneered an entirely new concept—funding these books through the sale of corporate profiles."

Cherbo honed his leading edge in Chicago, where he owned a top advertising agency before moving into publishing. Armed with a degree in business administration from Northwestern University, a mind that never stopped, and a keen sense of humor, Cherbo set out to succeed— and continues to do just that.

Cherbo Publishing Group (CPG), formerly a wholly owned subsidiary of

Jostens, Inc., a Fortune 500 company, has been a privately held corporation since 1993. CPG is North America's leading publisher of quality custom books for commercial, civic, historical, and trade associations. Publications range from hardcover state, regional, and commemorative books to softcover state and regional business reports. The company is headquartered in Encino, California, and operates regional offices in Philadelphia, Minneapolis, and Houston.

About CPG Publications

CPG has created books for some of America's leading organizations, including the U.S. Chamber of Commerce, Empire State Development, California Sesquicentennial Foundation, Chicago O'Hare International Airport, and the Indiana Manufacturers Association. Participants have included Blue Cross Blue Shield, DuPont, Toyota, Northrop Grumman, and Xerox.

CPG series range from history books to economic development/relocation books and from business reports to publications of special interest. The economic development series spotlights the outstanding economic and quality-of-life advantages of fast-growing cities, counties, regions, or states. The annual business reports provide an economic snapshot of individual cities, regions, or states. The commemorative series marks milestones for corporations, organizations, and professional and trade associations.

To find out how CPG can help you celebrate a special occasion, or for information on how to showcase your company or organization, contact Jack Cherbo at 818-783-0040, extension 26, or visit www.cherbopub.com.

Select CPG Publications

VISIONS OF OPPORTUNITY
City, Regional, and State Series

ALABAMA *The Progress, The Promise*

AMERICA & THE SPIRIT
OF ENTERPRISE
Century of Progress, Future of Promise

AURORA, ILLINOIS *A City Second to None*

CALIFORNIA *Golden Past, Shining Future*

CHATTANOOGA *The Renaissance of a City*

CINCINNATI *Bridges to the Future*

CONNECTICUT *Chartered for Progress*

DELAWARE *Incorporating Vision in Industry*

FORT WORTH *Where the Best Begins*

GREATER PHOENIX *Expanding Horizons*

JACKSONVILLE *Where the Future Leads*

LEHIGH VALLEY *Crossroads of Commerce*

MICHIGAN *America's Pacesetter*

MILWAUKEE *Midwestern Metropolis*

MISSOURI *Gateway to Enterprise*

NASHVILLE *Amplified*

NEW YORK STATE *Prime Mover*

NORTH CAROLINA *The State of Minds*

OKLAHOMA *The Center of It All*

PITTSBURGH *Smart City*

SOUTH DAKOTA *Pioneering the Future*

TOLEDO *Access. Opportunity. Edge.*

UTAH *Life Elevated*

WEST VIRGINIA *Reaching New Heights*

LEGACY
Commemorative Series

ALBERTA AT 100 *Celebrating the Legacy*

BUILD IT & THE CROWDS WILL COME
Seventy-Five Years of Public Assembly

CELEBRATE SAINT PAUL
150 Years of History

DAYTON *On the Wings of Progress*

THE EXHIBITION INDUSTRY
The Power of Commerce

IDAHO *The Heroic Journey*

MINNEAPOLIS *Currents of Change*

NEW YORK STATE ASSOCIATION
OF FIRE CHIEFS
Sizing Up a Century of Service

ROCHESTER, MINNESOTA
Transforming the World: Rochester at 150

VIRGINIA
Catalyst of Commerce for Four Centuries

VISIONS TAKING SHAPE
*Celebrating 50 Years of the Precast/
Prestressed Concrete Industry*

ANNUAL BUSINESS REPORTS
MINNESOTA REPORT *2007*

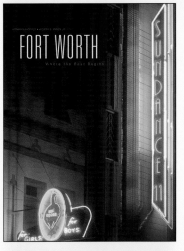
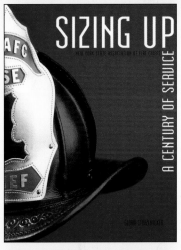
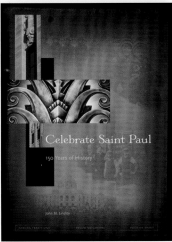
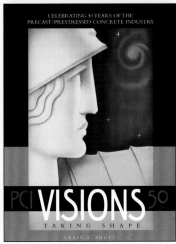
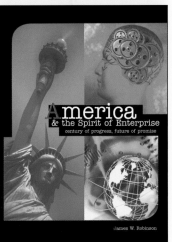

PHOTO CREDITS

cherbo publishing group, inc.

TYPOGRAPHY

Principal faces used: Univers, designed by Adrian Frutiger in 1957;
Helvetica, designed by Matthew Carter, Edouard Hoffmann,
and Max Miedinger in 1959

HARDWARE

Macintosh G5 desktops, digital color laser printing with Xerox Docucolor 250, digital
imaging with Creo EverSmart Supreme

SOFTWARE

QuarkXPress, Adobe Illustrator, Adobe Photoshop, Adobe Acrobat, Microsoft Word,
Eye-One Pro by Gretagmacbeth, Creo Oxygen, FlightCheck

PAPER

Text Paper: #80 Luna Matte

Bound in Rainbow® recycled content papers from
Ecological Fibers, Inc.

Dust Jacket: #100 Sterling-Litho Gloss